Self-Esteem
for Tots to Teens

Self-Esteem
for Tots to Teens

How you can help your children
feel more confident and lovable

Eugene Anderson, Ed.D.
George Redman, Ph.D.
Charlotte Rogers, Ph.D.

Second Edition, Revised and Expanded

Parenting & Teaching
Publications

Publisher's Cataloging in Publication
(Prepared by Quality Books, Inc.)

Anderson, Eugene, 1936-
  Self-esteem for tots to teens : how you can help your children feel
more confident and lovable / Eugene Anderson, George Redman,
Charlotte Rogers. — 2nd ed., rev. and expanded —
  p. cm.
  Includes bibliographical references and index.
  ISBN 1-879276-00-3

  1. Child rearing. 2. Child psychology. 3. Self-respect in children.
I. Redman, George, 1941- II. Rogers, Charlotte, 1940- III. Title.

HQ772   649.1
                                    QBI91-128

Library of Congress Catalog Card Number: 90-92130

Published by Parenting & Teaching Publications, Inc.,
16686 Meadowbrook Lane, Wayzata, MN 55391

96 95 94 93 92 91 10 9 8 7 6 5 4 3 2

Printed in the United States of America

Cover Illustration: Dwight Walles

Cover Design: Jennifer L. Nelson

Text Design: Anne Marie Hoppe

Editor: Kerstin Gorham

Production Manager: Patsey Kahmann

Typesetting: Stephen A. Lenius

To our lovable and capable children,
for whom we have much affection and esteem:

Eric, Jonathan, and Stephen
Ryan and Angela
Paige and Alex

and

To our spouses, who have contributed
immeasurably to the well-being of our children
and each one of us:

Judy
Shari
Hank

Table of Contents

Preface

Over and over again, it has been demonstrated that a sense of self-worth is critical to learning and growing and living. Children who believe they are competent and worthy develop an "I-can-do-it" attitude for coping with the problems and frustrations of life. Their positive concept of self helps them develop into strong, caring, responsible, compassionate human beings. On the other hand, children who are unable to view themselves as competent and worthwhile are prevented from living fulfilled and meaningful lives, and they also have difficulty helping others do the same.

Researchers and other professionals have noted a correlation between low self-esteem and a number of serious problems experienced by young people today. Among them are low academic achievement, juvenile delinquency, drug addiction, teenage pregnancy, eating disorders, depression, and suicide. We can help our children avoid these problems by fostering their self-esteem.

In this book we recommend five principles for building self-esteem in children. These principles must be applied with an understanding that children are not adults in little bodies, and, furthermore, that they differ from each other depending on their stage of development and unique personality. These differences must be taken into consideration as we nurture our children step-by-step toward mature adulthood.

Our book is organized in the following way: In the introduction we present five psychological characteristics youngsters possess and introduce the five principles for building self-esteem. Part I consists of five chapters that illustrate how to apply each of these principles. In each chapter we provide what we call vignettes—stories of typical family situations that positively or negatively affect self-esteem. Each vignette also includes some general guidelines for building self-esteem that relate to the principle highlighted. After the vignettes in each of the first four chapters we also provide a set of communication skills for carrying out the principle addressed and list some developmental needs of children that parents should consider. Each chapter closes with a summary. In Part II we show parents how to plan a systematic program for promoting self-esteem in their children.

Those who read the first edition of *Self-Esteem for Tots to Teens* told us that the book made them much more aware of building self-esteem in their children and significantly more able to do so. Teachers and others who work with children also told us that the book helped them immensely. In this expanded and revised edition we provide more vignettes concerning the early childhood and teenage years and highlight the communication skills necessary to carry out each self-esteem principle. You should find this new edition useful in working with children of all ages.

Our strong concern for building self-esteem in young people springs from several sources: parenting our own children, teaching and counseling students in public schools, formally preparing for our professional careers as educators and counselors, and offering self-esteem workshops and courses for parents, teachers, and other professionals. Preceding and underlying these experiences, the lessons and examples of our parents, schools, churches, and communities taught us to value the dignity and worth of all people—including children.

We hope our book will intensify your concern for building self-esteem in your children. What you do to help your children feel worthwhile will assist them in fulfilling their seemingly inborn drive towards competence and mastery, and will help them develop the inner strength they need to cope with the problems of growing up in an increasingly complex and challenging world.

Introduction

You undoubtedly know some children who are

- insecure about trying anything new
- overly self-conscious
- excessively fearful
- dominated by peers
- always trying to call attention to themselves
- overly anxious
- underachieving

Research findings tell us that children who persistently exhibit some or all of these characteristics lack self-esteem. That is, they have a self-image that is unsatisfactory to them because they lack the two essential components of self-esteem: self-confidence and self-respect.

How do children come to have low or high self-esteem? To a great extent, they learn it from their environment. As they interact with people and things around them, they continually receive new information and gather new insights about themselves, leading them to maintain or change their sense of self-worth. If the feedback is constantly negative, their self-esteem will likely be low. If it conveys to them that they have worth, their self-esteem will tend to be high.

Since the way we interact with our children is so important in shaping their self-esteem, it is critical that we invest time learning effective ways to communicate with them. Children need the kind of communication from us that not only helps them learn and grow, but also stimulates them to feel good about themselves.

Children Are Different from Adults

The first step in helping our youngsters develop a sense of self-worth is to understand how they view the world, and then to accept their view as appropriate for them at their stage of development. Children reason differently than adults do. They quite often cannot think of anybody but themselves, and they sometimes have difficulty planning ahead and remembering what they have been told. While this may frustrate us, we cannot drastically or quickly change the way children make sense out of the world. With the help of parents, children will start reasoning differently when they reach the appropriate stage of development. It's crucial that we understand this, for it will also affect the degree of satisfaction or disappointment we'll feel when the expectations we have for our children are either met or not met. Consider this illustration: A mother had taken her young son to McDonald's as a special treat. When she had finished her drink, she asked him for a sip of his. The child refused, saying that the drink was his. She protested that he should share, but he wouldn't give in. Realizing that her approach was wrong, she decided to try to think as the boy did and understand how he viewed the world at his stage of development. Realizing that he was naturally protective about what belonged to him, she offered to trade a french fry for a sip of his drink, and he smilingly concurred. She then praised him for his "generosity."

The young child here was behaving in a natural way for his level of development. To say this is not to condone self-centeredness but simply to assert a fact about young, developing children. Offering a trade-off to the child was appropriate for his developmental level because it made him feel he was getting something out of the deal. Praising him for his generosity, even though it was not fully developed, was a stimulus to help him grow into a truly generous person. Accepting his self-centeredness and yet providing a positive incentive to grow beyond it represent positive efforts on the mother's part to enhance the self-esteem of her child.

Children are not adults in little bodies! They have characteristics of their own, and we must respond to them as they are rather than as we would like them to be.

How Children Are Different from Mature Adults

s you work to build your children's self-esteem, keep the following five psychological characteristics of children in mind:

1. Children tend to be impulsive. They want what they want—and they want it now! At early stages, they are unable to delay gratification, even for a short time. They do not have a great deal of control over their feelings and bodies, they tend to focus all of their thoughts and feelings on the present, and they do not naturally worry about doing or saying the "wrong thing at the wrong time."

2. Children tend to be self-centered. Most parents want their children to grow up able to take the needs of others into account. Yet all of us started out self-centered and able to think only of ourselves. Children are the center of their own world. They are naturally "selfish." "Good" is what gives them pleasure; "bad" is what causes pain. As they develop, they become more willing to consider others, but only (at first) if they get something in return. Since a self-focused perspective is normal and unavoidable in children, we must accept this fact and therefore accept them. We emphasize, however, that we do not need to allow all the behavior that this self-focused perspective engenders.

3

3. Children tend to think in concrete and simple terms.
By "concrete," we mean that children think in terms of objects they can see and touch and sounds they can hear: they experience life through their senses. As a result, they have difficulty grasping ideas that are not conveyed by concrete examples. A recent study found that fourth graders share a concept of "mother" that's based on what they can see her doing—she "takes me shopping," she "bakes cookies," and she "goes to work." By contrast, mature adolescents and adults tend to describe "mother" in a more abstract way—in terms of what she *is* rather than *does*. She "is kind but firm," she "is more rigid than she would like to be," and she "respects the ideas of others." Unlike younger children, older, more mature young people can connect one idea with another without reference to concrete experience.

Children also think simply. They demonstrate this in many ways. They see things as black or white, good or bad, fine or not fine, but nothing in-between. They also take what adults say literally. For example, a child may interpret literally a parent's comment about having stayed at the party "until the last dog was hung"! In addition, young children tend to believe that what someone else gains, they must lose. "If Mom loves my sister a lot," a young child might think, "there will not be enough left over for me." Also, it is not uncommon for children to place blame on others, see only one cause for something, and focus on the immediate rather than the long-range or underlying causes. Finally, young children cannot readily put themselves in the shoes of others.

4. Children tend to seek rewards and avoid punishment.
For example, they will go to bed early to get a story read to them. They will do their household chores to get stars on a job chart. They will color a picture to earn praise from their parents. And they will wear a certain style of clothing to be accepted by their peers. We may sometimes wish our children were less depend-

ent on rewards, but we have to accept the fact they they're naturally motivated by what's in it for them.

At the same time, children tend to avoid the discomfort of punishment. In order to avoid punishment, they will sometimes fail to tell the truth, blame others, stay away from their parents, and try to talk their way out of a situation. While this sometimes frustrates us, we must recognize that it's natural for them at their stage of development.

5. Children tend to be easily influenced by their environment. If there is a mud puddle, they will step in it. If candy is around, they will eat it. If the gang decides to sneak off and go fishing, they will go too. Unlike mature adults, children find it hard to resist the attractions of their surroundings.

Parents play a significant part in the environment of their children. Young children love and admire their parents in ways they cannot even express, and they try to imitate their behavior. They also think *their* parents can do anything better than anyone else's parents.

As children approach and move into adolescence, peer groups start to exert a strong influence on them. At this stage, children want to dress and look like their friends and conform to the desires of the group. Peer-group influence, as we know, can be positive or negative. In either case, we should recognize that it's natural for children to feel this influence. To be insensitive to this reality may lead to unnecessary confrontations and harm our relationships with our children as well as their self-esteem.

Child Development Occurs in Stages

As they move through various stages of development, children will display, in varying degrees, the characteristics described above. At an early stage of development, for example, children are more impulsive than children at a later stage, and their thinking is more concrete and simplistic.

Because each developmental step that children take represents another necessary step toward mature adulthood, we must let them experience life in a way that's appropriate at that stage, as the mother did in the McDonald's illustration. We need to accept them as they are at the moment, as well as encourage them to move on, realizing that what our children are like at one stage of development is not what they will be like at a later stage. Knowing this should give us hope and encouragement, and it should caution us against being overly critical of normal childhood behavior.

Children Are Unique

We have just emphasized that children are different from adults and from other children at different stages of development. We must now point out what all of us also know from experience: each child is in many ways unique. We must, therefore, consider the individual tastes, fears, temperaments, interests, and abilities of our children as we attempt to build their self-esteem.

Five Principles for Raising Confident Children

Understanding the nature of children provides a foundation on which you can base your efforts to help them feel good about who they are and what they can do. We strongly believe that you will be successful if you follow five basic principles of self-esteem. In Part I, we describe these principles more fully and show you how to put them to use. Below we touch briefly on each of them and provide a rationale for its inclusion.

1. Listen to and acknowledge the thoughts and feelings of your children. When we do such things as take time to listen to our children, give them our full attention when they talk, empathize with them, and paraphrase their thoughts or feelings, we communicate that we accept them and that they count.

2. Structure situations to help your children experience feelings of success, not failure. Before our children get themselves into a jam and fail, we can structure situations so they have a greater chance to succeed at what they're trying to do. Here's one example: A young child is trying to throw a ball into a basket her father is holding. As she throws the ball, her father moves the basket to catch the ball and then says, "Good shot!" This extreme example illustrates how we can actively help children succeed by the conditions we set up for them. By setting clear and appropriate expectations, providing a reasonable amount of help and adequate incentives, and removing some of the obstacles to success, we can do much to foster feelings of success.

3. Give your children a feeling of reasonable control over their lives. By nature children need and desire to control their environment. When thwarted from doing so, they feel frustrated and inadequate. Some of us, however, don't let our children have enough control. By overprotecting children, we communicate to them that they are inadequate. Over time, they may come to feel increasingly powerless. Eventually, their sense of purposefulness may be reduced. Of course, it is also possible to give children too much control, leaving them feeling neglected and insecure. Giving children a feeling of reasonable control over their lives will help them feel lovable and capable.

4. Reinforce your children as lovable and capable. Reinforcing your children as lovable and capable means that you strengthen psychologically their belief that they are worthy to be

7

loved and that they are competent. Common ways of reinforcing children include praising them for what they do, hugging them, offering them tangible rewards, and directly telling them that you love them. Children cannot get enough positive reinforcement.

5. Model a positive view of yourself to your children. This is a sobering principle because it implies that our children can "catch" self-esteem from us by the degree of self-esteem we model to them. While we cannot totally control how we feel about ourselves, we can control, to some degree, how we talk about ourselves and how we react to the circumstances of life. Modeling healthy self-esteem to children is vital to their developing healthy self-esteem.

Summary

It is critical for the lifelong welfare of our children that we invest time and effort in building their self-esteem. We believe that we can best help our children by understanding their psychological characteristics and then applying the five basic principles of self-esteem. In the first part of this book, we will expand upon each of these principles and illustrate how they can be applied.

Children are not adults
in little bodies.

*We must respond to them
as they are rather than
as we would like them to be
and then step-by-step
nurture their growth.*

PART I

The Five Principles of Self-Esteem

Principle One

Listen to and Acknowledge the Thoughts and Feelings of Your Children

One of the major cries of youth is that they want to be heard and understood. In order to feel that they count and that they have something significant to offer in life, children need for parents and other caring adults to listen to them and acknowledge their thoughts and feelings. When children really feel they have been heard, they will not only feel more lovable and capable, but will also move more quickly to mature behavior.

As parents, however, we may feel inclined to instruct, advise, and evaluate our children rather than listen to and understand them. We want the best for our children and often believe that what we have to say to them is much more important than what they have to say to us. In addition, some of us are eager to turn our lively little children into socially acceptable creatures, and we are convinced that the way to accomplish this is to correct what we don't like. So we tend to tell our kids what they should feel and think. If what is actually on their minds does not fit with what we think should be there, we tell them that, too, leaving them with the early impression that they don't think and feel the way they should; they are not what they ought to be.

Rather than so quickly instructing, advising, and evaluating our children, we should concentrate instead on acknowledging their thoughts and feelings. Acknowledging the thoughts and feelings of children is not necessarily the same as approving of them, and it does not imply that we be permissive and let our children have their own way. It is simply a way of saying to our children that we understand and empathize with their thoughts and feelings.

What follows are vignettes that illustrate this principle. Some show what parents should do; some show what they shouldn't do.

Early Childhood

A Little "Pick-Me-Up" Helps

Judy Hill was a warm, caring, and responsive parent to her six-month-old daughter, Kristin. Every chance she had she would hold and cuddle Kristin, smile at her when she smiled, entertain her, and empathize with her various feelings. When she thought that Kristin was hungry, she would feed her.

One day when a neighbor friend was visiting, Kristin began to cry. Knowing that she had just eaten and that her diaper was dry, Judy picked Kristin up and comforted her. Immediately she stopped crying.

"You know something, Judy," her friend said. "You're a very caring, sensitive person, but you're going to reinforce Kristin's crying if you keep picking her up every time she cries. You don't want her to grow up crying at the least little thing, do you?"

"I don't think that will happen," Judy responded. "At her age I believe she needs all of the love and attention she can get."

Reflections

Judy did what a number of specialists in child development would have recommended she do. These experts tell us that infants need to know that their primary care-givers are steady, dependable, and there for them. Further, they claim that warm, sensitive care does not create dependency. Rather, it liberates children and enables them to become automonous and to securely explore their world.

While it is essential that we encourage our children to be less self-focused and impulsive, this can be done after a secure foundation has been established during infancy. Consistent, responsive care to children during the initial phase of their childhood will help them feel loved and worthy of care. Both are essential for self-esteem.

Guidelines for Building Self-Esteem

- Err on the side of being responsive to the demands of very young children. Responsive care will help them feel that their needs and wants have been heard and that they are therefore worthy of esteem.

"Water Won't Hurt You"

Don Martin decided to introduce his twenty-month-old, Chad, to the swimming pool. As Don stepped into the pool with him, Chad began to whimper. Then someone splashed water on them, and he began to fuss even more.

"Stop crying, Chad," his father said. "The water won't hurt you. You like to take baths and this is just the same!"

With that, he reached down and splashed water in the face of his now-screaming child.

Reflections

Chad was expressing fear to his father, but he wasn't listening. He couldn't understand what his father said, and his actions indicated that he did not think swimming was just like bathing. His father apparently didn't want to hear that he was afraid, so instead of sitting on the edge of the pool and allowing Chad to get accustomed to the new experience, he ignored his baby's message at a cost to his self-esteem.

Guidelines for Building Self-Esteem

- Be open and responsive to nonverbal messages from your children. They don't have to be able to talk to express feelings.
- Don't push your children into new experiences prematurely. Look for expressions of interest and readiness from them.

"It Serves You Right"

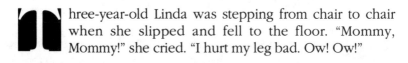 hree-year-old Linda was stepping from chair to chair when she slipped and fell to the floor. "Mommy, Mommy!" she cried. "I hurt my leg bad. Ow! Ow!"

"It serves you right," her mother said coldly. "I told you not to walk on those chairs. Now if you're going to cry about it, go to your room."

Reflections

Linda's mother committed an error in listening called "hard-heartedness." Rather than first responding with empathy (e.g., by saying, "That must really hurt"), she immediately reprimanded

Linda for not obeying. Such hard-hearted responses offered over time can lead children to believe that they are not valued or, even worse, that they are not wanted.

Guidelines for Building Self-Esteem

- Show your children that you are listening to them by expressing empathy and concern even when they get hurt doing something you didn't want them to do. When you do, they will feel loved and worthwhile.

"Maybe We Could Kill All the Babies"

Keisha Simms, age five, and her dad were discussing a news item about the recent death of a public figure. "Wouldn't it be nice if no one ever had to die?" wondered Keisha.

"Yeah, it sure would," her father replied. "But if that happened, we would have to do something because there would be too many people on Earth."

"Maybe we could kill all the babies," said Keisha.

"You know, in some countries they have killed babies for that very reason. Is that something you think people should do?" her father asked.

"No, I guess not. It would be too sad," said Keisha.

"I guess killing babies would make me awfully sad, too," said her father.

17

Reflections

Keisha's response about killing all the babies illustrates the simple logic and honesty that characterize the thinking of young children. Her father wisely did not squelch her comments. To reject them too quickly and strongly might have inhibited Keisha from offering ideas in the future. It might also have made her feel that something was wrong with her. Helping Keisha clarify her feelings led her to move to a more satisfactory conclusion and, at the same time, kept her self-esteem intact.

Guidelines for Building Self-Esteem

- Accept your children's thoughts by encouraging them to talk more about them.
- Do not reject too hastily the ideas that your children express, even when they are inconsistent with your adult standards.

"No, You Don't Wish That"

Sally Metcalf, a bouncing six-year-old, returned home one day from a birthday party with several kinds of candy, which she proceeded to eat. Since she wasn't usually allowed to eat much candy, she said to her mother, "I wish I never had to eat vegetables or meat or anything but cookies and candy. I could just live on cookies and candy!"

Her mother replied, "No, you don't wish that. You would be very unhealthy and have decayed teeth and no energy at all. Sweets are not good for you." Sally's face fell. "I still like candy," she protested.

Reflections

Sally's mother failed to acknowledge her child's desire to eat cookies and candy. She even discounted Sally's right to wish for sweets by saying, "No, you don't wish that." To reject Sally's right to wish was, in a way, to reject her as a person.

If Sally's mother had said, "Sometimes it might seem like you'd never get tired of eating cookies and candy, doesn't it?" Sally might have replied, "Yes, but I know a lot of candy isn't good for me."

If Sally hadn't come to this conclusion and her mother had thought it was an opportune time to talk with her about the harmful effects of eating too many sweets, Sally would have been more receptive to what her mother had to say, since her mother had first listened to her.

Guidelines for Building Self-Esteem

- Acknowledge what your children are thinking and feeling even if it seems irrational or illogical to you. One good way of doing this is to paraphrase what they have expressed to you. Remember, acknowledging what your children are thinking or feeling is not the same as condoning what they say.
- Do not feel compelled to lecture and "teach a lesson" to your children at every turn, especially when emotions are running high.

Middle Childhood

"Thank You for Sharing Your Room"

Seven-year-old Tina Kurtz had the largest bedroom in the house, so whenever the family had guests, she had to give up her room and move in with her sister. Days before Grandma and Grandpa or Aunt Linda and Uncle Dave were due to visit, she would start complaining: "Why do I have to be the one to give up my room? Why me? It's not fair. My clothes will have to be moved. Let them sleep somewhere else."

As Tina grew angry and frustrated, her mother would listen to and talk about her child's feelings: "I know it's very inconvenient for you, Tina. I'm sorry you have to lend your room. I'll help you clean it, and I'll help you move some clothes to your sister's room. Thank you for sharing your room."

While she didn't really like sharing her room, Tina did enjoy moving her clothes and cleaning her room with her mother.

Reflections

Tina's thoughts and feelings were normal for a child her age (although many children might not express these thoughts to a parent and would feel ashamed and angry over the feelings). Tina's mother did not take the permissive way out and allow her to keep her room, but she didn't get angry either or make Tina ashamed of feeling the way she did. She accepted Tina's feelings and then got her to cooperate in getting her room ready for guests, knowing that someday Tina wouldn't mind sharing.

Guidelines for Building Self-Esteem

- Since children are not born generous, do not constantly point out their lack of generosity. Doing so will only instill shame and anger and keep them at an egocentric level for a longer period of time. Instead, indicate that you understand their self-centered interests.
- Acknowledge the thoughts and feelings of your children by expressing empathy. Doing so will help them feel empowered and move them more rapidly toward consideration of others.

"You Felt Frustrated?"

The Hernandez family had spent the day at a family reunion. On the way home, daughter Tracey, age eight, said, "I'm mad at Aunt Rita, and I don't know if I like her anymore. She made me hug and kiss her and I didn't want to—and she asked me a question and never listened to the answer."

Tracey's mother replied, "You felt frustrated with Aunt Rita today, is that it?"

"Yes," said Tracey. "She made me mad. Sometimes grown-ups make me sick."

Reflections

Children are impulsive and honest if allowed to be. There is no human being who hasn't felt frustration and anger at a relative or friend at some time. Children should have someone to whom they can honestly express negative feelings without shame and guilt. Their self-esteem will be enhanced if they realize that occasionally everyone has thoughts like these.

Guidelines for Building Self-Esteem

- Allow your children to express negative as well as positive feelings. To say, "You shouldn't feel that way," "It's bad," or "It's not nice," negatively affects a child's image of herself. Children mature faster when you encourage them to examine and express their feelings honestly.

Overkill

One evening, just before dinner, seven-year-old Andrew Eisner, a carefree, curious, and energetic child, let it be known that he and his eight-year-old brother, Aaron, had been "splitting" some trees behind their house. His father, filled with the vision that all of their neighbor's backyard trees had been flattened, demanded, "You weren't near John Heglund's new trees, were you?" Andrew wasn't sure.

"What do you mean, you're not sure?" his father responded. "Don't you know that trees are expensive, and it takes a long time for trees to grow? You know you could end up having to spend half of your savings to pay for the damaged trees!" Andrew's only response was that he wasn't the only one. Aaron had hacked down three trees, and his friend Chris had leveled two more.

Realizing that he needed to find out more specifically what had happened, his father asked with more openness, "What happened, Andrew?"

Andrew replied, "We took a dead limb and scraped some bark off of five sumac trees."

"Let's go and look at the situation," his father responded.

Reflections

Parents often too quickly imagine the worst when something happens. Andrew's father's reaction communicated that he thought the boys were capable of destroying all of their neighbor's trees, and his tone of voice conveyed a guilty verdict before the facts were known. This could only communicate distrust to the boys and damage their sense of self-worth. Fortunately, Andrew's father realized he needed to listen to the boys rather than getting upset so quickly and asked the open question, "What happened, Andrew?"

Guidelines for Building Self-Esteem

- Show your children you respect them by listening to them rather than hastily judging them or creating the "worst scenario" before you know the facts.
- Show your children that you are interested in their thoughts and feelings by asking open questions that draw them out.
- Be calm when you are talking with your children about a crisis that has arisen. Your behavior will help them learn to assume a similar attitude when they experience crises in their own lives.

Different Strokes

David Lahr was excited about his ninth birthday party. He and his ten-year-old brother, Mike, went with their mother to the store to buy small toys, chewing gum, and noisemakers for the guests. When they returned, the two boys arranged the favors at each guest's place at the table.

"I wish I could keep all of these for myself," said David. "I wish I didn't have to give them to the people at my party."

"Just seeing all of these goodies makes you want them for yourself, doesn't it?" responded his mother. "But just think— you'll be getting presents from all your friends, and they'll be so happy to get these favors from you.

"Yeah, Dave," said Mike, "it wouldn't be very nice to keep all this stuff for yourself. Think how bummed out the other guys would be if they didn't get anything."

"Yes," said their mother, "the guests will be very happy and grateful to David when they see all the trouble he has taken to get these favors for them."

Reflections

Dave and Mike were about the same age, but Mike was a little ahead of Dave in considering others. Since Dave was still fairly focused on the "here and now" and quite opportunistic, giving away the favors didn't make much sense to him until his mother reminded him that he would be "rewarded" for his generosity— his friends would bring him gifts. Mike was more interested in pleasing other people and would have given away the favors because it was the "nice thing to do." Their mother appropriately responded differently to each boy.

Guidelines for Building Self-Esteem

- Remember that even children close in age may be at different levels of development and see the world quite differently.
- Recognize that being generous means very little to children at a self-centered stage unless they get something in return.

Burst Balloon

Eight-year-old Jennifer McGrath and her family had just returned from a 500-mile trip to visit Grandma. On their way to Sunday School the next day, Jennifer, a withdrawn girl who usually didn't express her thoughts or feelings freely, exclaimed enthusiastically, "I wish we could take a trip to Grandma's in an electric car!"

Her father quickly responded, "But you would run out of electricity before you got there!" Jennifer suddenly stopped talking and shrank back into her own quiet world of contemplation.

Reflections

Jennifer's father missed a golden opportunity to hear what his daughter had to say and to affirm her for being willing to express herself. Because of her insecurity, Jennifer may have interpreted her father's response not only as a rejection of her idea, but also as a rejection of herself.

Instead of "bursting a child's balloon" so quickly, her father might have shown support for his daughter's idea by saying, "That's an interesting idea." Then he could have openly asked, "What is it about an electric car that makes you excited about driving one to Grandma's?" Such a question might have stimulated Jennifer to expand on her thoughts and made her feel that she counted in her father's eyes.

Guidelines for Building Self-Esteem

- Show your children that you are listening to them by asking open questions. Such questions allow them to talk more and explain things from their point of view.
- Respond positively to ideas your children express, even if they may not be complete or practical.

How Does It Benefit Me?

he Davis family (including Rama, twelve, and Kiah, seven) was to be interviewed by a graduate student in sociology for a term paper on different family structures. When the student arrived, she brought the family a quart of chocolate mint ice cream, telling the children that it was a gift for them. After she was gone and they were eating the ice cream, Kiah said, "That lady sure was nice. She brought my favorite kind of ice cream."

"Is that why you think she was nice?" Rama said. "Just because she brought ice cream?"

"Yes," said her puzzled sister.

Rama continued, "What has that got to do with her being nice? Just because—"

Looking at Kiah, their father interrupted, "Yes, she was nice, wasn't she? And it was lucky she brought your favorite kind of ice cream."

Reflections

Kiah's comments show that she was at a very opportunistic stage of development, where "nice" means "nice to me" and "good" means "makes me feel good." Rama's stage of development was more advanced: she judged people's "niceness" more on their personal qualities. Their father was wise to intervene and accept Kiah's feelings for what they were. There was no reason to allow Rama to hurt and confuse Kiah just because she didn't have a more mature way of deciding what "nice" was. Kiah's feelings were appropriate for her age and stage of development.

Guidelines for Building Self-Esteem

- Listen carefully for indications of your children's stage of intellectual, social, and moral development.
- Affirm your children for having thoughts and feelings that are reasonable for their stage of development.

Susan's Birthday Present

S usan's eleventh birthday had arrived, and her father had bought her a pretty charm for her bracelet. When she opened the gift, however, she looked a little disappointed but thanked her father graciously. Her father smiled, then gently said, "Do you like it, honey? Are you sure it was what you wanted?"

Susan hesitated, then said, "Daddy, it's just that I really wanted a different charm. I've had my eye on it for a long time; the one with the four-leaf clover."

Her father said, "What I wanted was to get you something you would really like. We'll go back tomorrow and exchange this one for the four-leaf-clover charm."

"Are you sure it's all right?" Susan asked.

"Of course," he said. "If the store allows changes, we'll return it for the one you wanted."

"Oh, Dad, thanks," she said gratefully. "You're terrific!"

Reflections

Susan felt so comfortable with her father that when he asked her how she liked the gift, she could honestly tell him she was disappointed. Pleasing her was more important to her father than guessing correctly about what to give her. His behavior is an excellent example of the kind of open acceptance that is so critical to enhancing self-esteem.

Guidelines for Building Self-Esteem

- Listen openly to the needs and interests of your children. This is an excellent way to show them they are important to you.
- Whenever possible and prudent, meet the expressed needs and interests of your children.

Teens

To Flip or Not to Flip

t dinner one evening thirteen-year-old Jessica said to her mother, "I'm not sure if I should try out for the gymnastic team."

"I think you should," her mother urged her encouragingly. "I've seen you do back flips, and you're great. You would make an excellent member of the team."

Reflections

At first glance, Jessica's mother's response seems positive and supportive. Yet she made the mistake of advising too quickly rather than listening first. Jessica had a concern to share. Her mother did not pick up on it. Jessica's mother could have shown that she was listening by openly asking, "What is it that you are uncertain about?" After listening to Jessica express her concern, her mother could then have advised her to go out for the gymnastic team if she still thought it appropriate to do so.

Guidelines for Building Self-Esteem

- Show your children that you are hearing their concerns by asking clarifying questions that draw them out further.
- Listen to children before advising them. Sometimes, when no advice has been asked for, try not giving any at all.

"You All Have Interesting Ideas"

 nne, Lynn, and Maria, all thirteen, were talking with Maria's mother about growing up and becoming adults, which the three were eager to do.

"I just can't wait to grow up," said Anne. "I know I'll be a grown-up when I begin to have my period. Then I can have babies."

Lynn chimed in, "For me it'll be when I get a job and can earn my own money.

Maria thought for a moment and then offered, "I think you're not really a grown-up until you can think for yourself, but still respect authority."

"You all have interesting ideas," said Maria's mother.

Reflections

Although these three girls were the same age, they represented different levels of maturity. Each of their ideas made sense viewed from each girl's stage of development. Anne's thinking was still very concrete; she saw adulthood as a physical process that automatically changed you from girl to woman. Lynn, who was more developmentally mature, thought that taking on a socially accepted adult role (worker) constituted adulthood. Maria was the most abstract and complex thinker. For her, adulthood meant accepting the need to be both independent and dependent. Maria's mother wisely accepted each girl's point of view as appropriate for her level of development.

Guidelines for Building Self-Esteem

- Listen to your children in order to understand their particular stage of development.
- Accept the ideas of your children and then display a slightly more complex way of viewing the world (as Lynn did for Anne and Maria for Lynn). This will leave their self-esteem intact and at the same time encourage movement to a higher stage of psychological development.

"That's a Stupid Idea!"

One day while driving to the store with his father, fifteen-year-old Adam became interested in a radio report about a group of drug dealers in a nearby city. After a period of silence, Adam turned to his father and said, "Sometime I'd like to try drugs just to see what they're like."

His father snapped back, "Are you crazy? That's a stupid idea! Drugs can kill you."

The discussion came to an abrupt end and Adam did not bring up the topic with his father again.

Reflections

Adam, in his attempt to be open with his father, received strong judgment from him on two levels. Not only was his idea deemed stupid, he was labeled "crazy." Rather than being so judgmental, Adam's father should have encouraged him to elaborate on his thoughts. He could have done this by saying something like, "Tell me more about what you are thinking" or "What is there about trying drugs that makes you curious?"

31

Listening openly to Adam would have given him the feeling that his ideas were important and therefore he was important. It would also have given Adam's father a better basis for talking with him further about using drugs.

Guidelines for Building Self-Esteem

- Listen to your children rather than making impulsive judgments about them and their ideas.
- Show your children that you are interested in what they have to say by asking them to elaborate on their thoughts and feelings.
- Recognize that children sometimes state points of view for the purpose of thinking them through rather than arguing for and acting on them.

Communication Skills for Listening to and Acknowledging Thoughts and Feelings

Following are the most critical verbal communication skills for carrying out the listening and acknowledging principle. While there is no one correct way to carry out each skill, we provide an example or two of what you *might* say.

- **Paraphrase what children have said instead of evaluating it.** For example:

  Child says: I wish I didn't have to go to school today.
  Paraphrasing response: You'd rather be somewhere else than at school today?

Child says: Children don't need as much sleep as parents think they do. I could stay up later and still be OK the next day.

Paraphrasing response: You're feeling that you could get by on less sleep than we require you to have?

- **Show your children that you empathize with them.** For example:

  Child says: The coach yelled at me for missing a practice shot today. It made me mad when he yelled.

  Empathic response: I can see why you're mad at your coach. Nobody likes to be yelled at. I know I don't.

  Child Says: I wish I had more clothes. Some of my friends have tons of clothes.

  Empathic response: When I was in junior high, I wanted lots of new clothes, too. I think it's natural to want pretty things.

- **Ask open questions that allow children to "tell it like it is" from their point of view.** For example:

  Child says: I'd like to move the furniture around in my room.

  Open questioning response: How do you think it should be arranged?

  Child says: My grades are not as good as they were last quarter.

  Open questioning response: Why do you think they are lower?

- **Seek clarification of meaning.** For example:

  Child says: This homework is a bummer.

  Clarifying response: What do you mean when you say it's a bummer?

Child says: You're not fair with me.

Clarifying response: You say I'm unfair. What would be an example of what I do that you consider unfair?

Child says: We need to sign up for basketball today.

Clarifying response: Are you saying that you want me to go over to the school today and sign you up, or are you saying that you want to do it yourself?

- **Invite your children to elaborate on what they have told you.** For example:

Child says: We really had fun in school today.

Elaborating response: Tell me more about it.

Child says: When we were taking a shower after gym today, the fire alarm went off.

Elaborating response: That's interesting. Then what happened?

Developmental Needs of Children That Should Be Considered in Applying the Listening and Acknowledging Skills

Younger, less mature children need:

- an opportunity to express self-focused, self-protecting, and impulsive ideas, feelings, and behaviors.
- physical indications that you are listening to and acknowledging their thoughts and feelings (for example, allowing

them to cry on your shoulder, reflecting their emotional expressions, and giving them reasonable time to express their ideas and feelings).

Older, more mature children need:

- patient and nonjudgmental responses from you to the thoughts and feelings that often arise from peer-group perspectives.
- verbal, as well as physical, indications that you hear and accept what your children have to say (for example, paraphrasing their ideas and feelings, asking them to elaborate on their thoughts and emotions, and serving as consultants rather than decision-makers when your children talk with you).

Summary

The principle we've developed in this chapter requires that as a parent you cultivate an attitude of empathy and support. This attitude conveys that you want to build a relationship with your children and that your children are important to you. Exposure to this attitude helps children feel they have self-worth.

Every child has thoughts and feelings like those displayed by the children in our examples. Sadly, even very young children learn to hide their feelings and feel ashamed of having them. But these thoughts and feelings won't just disappear, and the cost to self-esteem is great when they are denied. We are not saying, "Let kids do as they please." We are saying, "Let what is inside your children be heard. Listen to them and accept them for who they are at every stage of their lives." Then proceed as parents to do what you think is best. Remember, you do not lose control when you listen to and acknowledge your children's feelings—you gain control because children gain respect for you and themselves.

*When children really feel
they've been heard,
they will not only feel more
lovable and capable, but
will also move more quickly
to mature behavior.*

Structure Situations to Help Your Children Experience Feelings of Success, Not Failure

For their self-esteem to be high, children need to feel successful. We sometimes, however, set our children up for failure. We may not do this intentionally, but we do it, and the failure that follows is often accompanied by parental reprimands, which amplify children's feelings of failure and lower their self-esteem.

How do some parents set their children up for failure?

1. By having inappropriate expectations. Parents sometimes expect small children to sit quietly for long periods of time, not to fuss when they're tired, and to stay clean when they play outside. In general, expecting adultlike behavior from children sets them up for failure.

2. By not making their expectations clear to their children. Parents may state their expectations in such general terms that their children don't know how to comply with them. For instance, telling a child to go up and clean his room is too general and incomplete if part of what you want him to do is dust the room.

3. By not providing attractive incentives. Failing to identify and offer attractive incentives for accomplishing a goal may account for a child's failure to achieve it. Not offering a reward for doing a task, for example, may explain why a youngster fails to get the job done.

4. By not providing enough help to their children, or by providing too much. While it is difficult to say what constitutes "too little" or "too much" help, we can say that it is important to listen to our children. They will let us know by their words or their expressions that they need more or less help. If a child looks defeated or frustrated, we may need to pitch in. If a child says firmly, "I can do it myself," we may need to back off.

5. By not removing obstacles to success or by not building in the kind of support that will help children succeed. Permitting the TV to be on when your child is studying may be an obstacle to success. Granting your child the use of your den for doing homework or buying a desk for her room provides support for getting the work done successfully.

6. By holding standards that are too high or too low. We can make our children fail by setting standards for their behavior that are beyond their abilities, such as expecting a three-year-old to ride a bicycle. We can also foster feelings of failure by not giving them enough of a challenge, such as expecting a fourth grader with a ninth-grade reading ability to get excited about a fourth-grade reading book. (This fourth grader may feel a sense of failure because his abilities are judged to be lower than they really are and because he does not feel the excitement that is expected.)

Rather than setting up our children for failure in one of these six ways, we should set them up for success by having appropriate and clear expectations, providing attractive incentives, offering the appropriate amount of help, removing obstacles and building in necessary supports, and holding reasonable standards for evaluating their performance.

What follows are vignettes and guidelines that highlight what to do and what not to do to set kids up for feelings of success rather than failure.

Early Childhood

Beyond Reach

Four-month-old Josh was playing with a sponge ball his parents had given him when it fell off his fingertips and rolled out of reach. Sadly gazing at the ball that seemed to have a mind of its own, Josh began to cry.

Reflections

Josh must have had strong feelings of frustration when he was unable to retrieve the ball. His parents could have structured the situation for success by giving him an object to play with that he could have controlled better, such as one that was easier to hold on to or one that wouldn't roll away. Or his parents could have ensured feelings of success by being there to retrieve the ball when necessary. Having better control would have helped Josh feel more capable.

Guidelines for Building Self-Esteem

- Increase feelings of success and reduce frustration for infants by providing them with toys that are easy to control and operate.
- Structure situations for success by giving infants help when they need it.

Through the Child's Eyes

he Washingtons were interested in providing a stimulating environment for their nine-month-old daughter, Shani. Putting themselves in Shani's diapers, they realized that as Shani lay in her crib, she could see only the bottom side of the animals hanging on her mobile. They decided to reposition the animals sideways so Shani could see their bodies and faces better. Shani spent many happy hours enjoying the new view of her animals.

Reflections

The Washingtons wisely considered Shani's perspective as they attempted to create a stimulating environment for her. Repositioning the animals so that Shani could see them better was a creative idea that surely made her viewing experience more pleasurable and contributed to her feelings of success by removing any frustration she may have felt at not being able to see the animals from a proper perspective.

Guidelines for Building Self-Esteem

- Carefully consider the perspective of small children as you do such things as position mobiles, pictures, and other objects for their enjoyment.

Reach Out and Touch Someone

One-year-old Michelle Robbins was learning to walk. For several days she had been able to take steps as long as she held on to something, like her father or a table. To encourage Michelle's progress, her father would hold out his hand and invite Michelle to step toward him, always carefully staying within reach. When Michelle began to fall, her father would quickly catch her and return her to her feet. As Michelle became able to take more steps without holding on, her father increased the distance between them. Each time Michelle reached her father successfully, she got a big hug and a kiss.

Reflections

While Michelle's father did what most of us would naturally do, his actions provide a simple illustration of this chapter's principle. He structured the situation for success by keeping a supporting hand close to Michelle and by catching her when she began to fall. He also immediately reinforced Michelle with a hug and a kiss, which, because of their physical form, were powerful reinforcers. Michelle's success and the praise she received significantly helped to launch her self-confidence.

Guidelines for Building Self-Esteem

- Help your children be successful by having them perform tasks that you are quite certain they are physically and mentally able to do.
- Adjust the degree of challenge or difficulty of a task according to your children's abilities.

- Without doing a task for your children, offer a helping hand when needed.
- Reinforce young children's successes with physical rewards, such as hugs and kisses.

"Come On, You're a Big Boy"

When Justin Lund was two years old, his father taught him to shake hands. Justin's father was so proud of his son's accomplishment that when a neighbor came to visit, he immediately asked Justin to demonstrate his skill. But Justin refused to perform for a stranger.

"Come on, you're a big boy. Shake hands," his father pleaded. But all Justin did was retreat to the security of his father's pant leg.

Reflections

In our attempts to show off what our children can do, we often inappropriately expect them to perform for others before they're ready. Justin apparently did not feel secure about demonstrating his newly learned social skill, so the experience had a negative effect on him and might have caused him to be self-conscious and reticent in the future.

Justin's father should have waited until a close friend of the family came to visit and then, after shaking hands with the friend himself, asked Justin if he would do likewise. If Justin had hesitated, his father should have withdrawn the request and assured him that it was OK not to perform.

Guidelines for Building Self-Esteem

- Before asking your children to perform for others, look for indications that they are eager, or at least willing, to show others what they have learned.
- Don't make your children self-conscious by continuing to push them to perform for others when they hesitate to do so.

"Bobby, Just Look at You!"

One Sunday, Bobby Holter's parents told their four-year-old son that he could play outside on the church grounds while they had a quick cup of coffee with other parishioners in Fellowship Hall. After the thirty-minute social gathering, the Holters went outside to retrieve Bobby. When they found him, he had grass stains on his pants, dirt smudges on his sport coat, and scuff marks on his recently polished shoes.

With a voice that could be heard at the far end of the parking lot, his father yelled, "Bobby, just look at you! I don't believe it. You've totally ruined the outfit Aunt Mary gave you. You ought to be ashamed of yourself. This will be the last time that you go outside after church." As Bobby got into the car, his father continued, "And just look at how red your face is from running around."

Reflections

Bobby's parents set him up for failure and criticism by allowing him to play outside in his best outfit. They had apparently assumed that Bobby had adult judgment and were holding him accountable for keeping clean. In fact, Bobby was just a typical child—adventuresome, curious, and unconcerned with cleanliness.

Also worth noting is the heavy burden of shame Bobby's father placed on him. Making Bobby feel ashamed of his behavior was not enough. He also had to throw in an extra jab about his red face.

Guidelines for Building Self-Esteem

- Avoid inappropriate expectations. Assume that young children do not have adult judgment and an adult sense of responsibility and structure your expectations and the environment accordingly.
- Make your expectations clear to your child.
- When disciplining children, avoid "dumping" on them when they are already down.

Middle Childhood

Greener Pastures

Chris Shimota, a playful six-year-old, was given the job of clipping grass around trees while her father and older brother mowed the lawn. For the first few minutes, Chris did pretty well, but then she slowed down and got easily distracted.

Deciding that Chris was bored rather than lazy, her father asked her if she'd like to mow a couple of strips of grass. Chris eagerly accepted the offer and then, after finishing this more challenging task, went back to clipping grass with gusto. When the yard work was completed, Chris's father treated his helpers to ice-cream cones.

Reflections

It's easy to decide that our kids are lazy when they don't stick to a task. But it's just as likely that they're either bored, overchallenged, or unable to recognize any incentive for continuing the job.

By inviting Chris to try her hand at mowing, her father gave her a sense of fulfillment and an incentive to continue her clipping more enthusiastically.

Getting an ice-cream cone when the job was done was the kind of reward that could stimulate Chris to do the lawn again next time, and the experience of going to get the cones together gave father and daughter another opportunity to build a good relationship.

Guidelines for Building Self-Esteem

- Offer your children new and more challenging responsibilities as a way of motivating them to work and to feel good about themselves.
- Offer your children incentives to do a task. Incentives will not only motivate them to accomplish the task but also communicate that you are concerned about their needs and interests.

Don't Worry about Spilled Milk

he Wongs let their two children, ages six and seven, take responsibility for aspects of their own care, such as preparing their own breakfast when they wanted cold cereal.

To improve the likelihood that their children would succeed, the Wongs structured the situation in several ways. They put the cold cereal and other necessities on lower shelves so the children could reach them without a chair. They bought unbreakable bowls, child-sized chairs, and a hard plastic table, which they set up on the linoleum so cleaning would be easy. They also strategically positioned the sponge and paper towels so that spills could be easily wiped up. Finally, before the children began to make their own breakfast, the Wongs demonstrated the steps involved.

On the first day that their children made breakfast, the Wongs watched carefully, offered advice, and generously praised each correct step. When something went wrong, they showed the children how to do it properly, avoiding punishment. As a result, the children learned well, felt pride in their new achievement, and grew confident that they could be responsible for making their own breakfast.

Reflections

The Wongs didn't expect that their children would automatically know how to perform an adult-level activity. They realized that preparing breakfast was difficult for young children, and that they would need to be taught how. They also realized the importance of structuring the environment in a way that helped ensure success rather than failure. They sensed that when their children learned how to make breakfast, they would become more self-confident and more willing to accept responsibility.

Guidelines for Building Self-Esteem

- Structure the physical environment of your children in a way that promotes success and minimizes failure. For young children, follow the K.I.S.S. system—Keep It Structured and Supportive.

- Teach your young children to do jobs they haven't done before, but give them time to practice. You increase the likelihood of failure if you assume that they naturally know how to do things you know how to do.

"Stay Around"

 ight-year-old Vinnie asked his mother if he could go out to play. His mother replied, "Yes, but stay around. We're going to have dinner soon."

When it was time to eat, his mother opened the door and called for Vinnie. He didn't come and didn't come. When he finally showed up ten minutes later, his mother was furious. "Where were you? I called three times and you didn't answer. You're not going out to play for the rest of the week."

Defending himself, Vinnie protested, "I was staying around. I didn't hear any calls."

Reflections

Vinnie's mother set him up for failure by not clearly indicating what she meant by "staying around." She could have told Vinnie to play within certain boundaries and not to go inside anyone's house. Doing so would have increased the chances that he would have been successful in getting home on time.

Guidelines for Building Self-Esteem

• Be clear and specific in expectations that you convey to or negotiate with your children. When needed, offer examples of what is expected.

A Chance to Reconsider

John Boren and Barry, his eight-year-old son, were shopping at the local department store. After picking up what he needed in the clothing department, John returned to where he had left his son. He noticed that Barry had taken off his sweater, rolled it into a ball, and was glancing around defensively. John thought Barry might be hiding a toy there.

Since he was not certain that Barry had actually taken something and since, to his knowledge, Barry had never stolen anything, John said to him, "You know, son, the way you're carrying that sweater could give people the impression that you've taken something and are hiding it there. It's cool enough in here to have your sweater on. I'm going over to the houseware department and when I come back, I want to see that sweater on you."

As he was walking away, John glanced back and noticed that Barry had unfolded his sweater and was putting a toy back on the shelf. When he had finished his errand and returned to the toy department, John said, "Thanks, Barry, for putting your sweater on. You know it is very important not to give other people the impression that we've taken something without paying for it. Let's go to the checkout register and pay for the items we want to buy."

Reflections

Like most of us, John wanted to raise an honest child. But he resisted trying directly to teach his son a lesson in honesty by accusing him (perhaps falsely) and then forcing him to prove his innocence or admit his guilt. Instead, he indirectly encouraged Barry to be honest by allowing him to reconsider and reverse his actions. John's strategy not only stimulated his son to be honest, it also helped preserve his self-esteem. Had Barry stolen the toy and not returned it, his father would have had to confront him.

Guidelines for Building Self-Esteem

- Give your children the opportunity to modify inappropriate or incorrect behavior before confronting them with it.
- Do not, without substantial evidence, accuse your children of wrongdoing. False accusations communicate distrust.

"You Figured It Out!"

Wendy White, an even-tempered nine-year-old, examined the dials, knobs, and words on the dashboard of her parents' car. She read, "On". . . "Off". . . "Fan". . . "Bilevel." "What does 'bilevel' mean?" she asked.

Deciding to challenge her daughter, Alice White threw the question back to her, saying, "I'll bet you can figure it out. What do you suppose 'bilevel' means?"

Wendy thought for a moment and said, "It seems to mean that hot air comes out at a certain level, either up here by the window or down on the floor."

"Right," her mother replied. "Now what do you suppose 'bi' means?"

"Hmm, I don't know," said Wendy.

"Can you think of any other words you know that begin with 'bi'?"

"Bicycle," Wendy quickly replied.

"Right. What do you think 'bi' means in bicycle . . . not tricycle but bicycle?" continued her mother.

"I know," said Wendy. "It means two wheels."

"Yes, two," said her mother. "Now what is bilevel?"

"Two levels?" asked Wendy uncertainly.

"Yes," her mother responded. "It means hot air comes out of both the top level and the bottom level at the same time. You figured it out. Great job!"

Reflections

Helping Wendy figure out the answer to her own question had at least two benefits for her. First, she learned the meaning of the prefix 'bi,' and second, and more important, she confirmed that she could successfully solve problems herself. The success and increased confidence could only enhance her self-esteem.

Guidelines for Building Self-Esteem

- Help your children answer simple questions or solve simple problems themselves. Encourage expanded thinking in children—stimulate them to ask and answer questions related to but beyond the original topic.

- Help your children relate new ideas to knowledge they already have.
- In guiding the learning of your young children, remember to use ideas and terms that are concrete rather than abstract, and break down a complex idea or skill into a number of smaller, achievable learning steps.

Brushing for Dollars

Nine-year-old Mark Shields seemed to regard a toothbrush as his natural enemy. His parents constantly had to remind him to brush his teeth. They hated to nag, and, to make matters even more frustrating, their preaching brought no improvement. Finally, his father created a colorful chart on which Mark could check off morning and evening brushings. Each time he brushed he got a nickel, so he could earn seventy cents a week if he didn't forget. Mark was delighted.

Reflections

Children often do not value what we value—for example, having healthy teeth. Mark's self-esteem must have suffered from the constant nagging of his parents. His parents' new approach gave him a reward for brushing that he understood, and at the same time it reinforced good dental habits. Habits instilled by concrete rewards will remain long after a child has grown up and the original reward is no longer important.

Guidelines for Building Self-Esteem

- Remember that children are oriented in the "here and now" and often need concrete, immediate, and attractive rewards to stimulate them to perform a necessary task.
- Don't use negative, nagging approaches. Nagging communicates mistrust and a lack of confidence in your children. Instead, use techniques that encourage and reward positive behavior and build your children's confidence.

"You've Got Five Minutes to Get Ready for Bed"

Matt, Nathaniel, and Rob Gale, ranging in age from six to nine, readily got up each morning, but would dilly-dally before bed at night. Their parents had tried several tactics to speed them up. One was the "timing game."

"You have five minutes to get your pajamas on, brush your teeth, and be in bed," they would announce. "Four minutes left; you'd better hurry. Sixty, fifty-nine, fifty-eight . . . five, four, three, two and a half . . . two . . . one and a half . . . one. Time's up!"

This game helped, but the boys continued to be relatively slow. Matt usually sat during most of the game and picked dirt from his toes. At the last minute, he would make a mad dash to get dressed, sometimes beating the deadline. Nathaniel spent so much time resisting the game that he hardly ever met the mark. Rob, the oldest brother, was usually in bed with his pajamas on after two minutes of competition, taunting his two younger brothers for being so slow.

On other nights, the Gales also tried offering the boys a story if they got ready for bed in time. As their sons continued to dawdle, they would warn, "Boys, remember, if you don't get ready in time, no story." "I guess you don't want a story." "You really don't want a story, do you?" "That's it. No story. Get in bed."

Reflections

There may be no foolproof way to encourage children to get ready for bed quickly and properly, but it is interesting to see how the two tactics the Gales employed affected the self-esteem of their children.

Children dress themselves at different speeds, depending on their varying stages of development and unique personalities. Evidently, the timing game so overwhelmed Nathaniel that he didn't want to play at all. Matt possibly thought that the time period was so long that he could wait and challenge the clock. The game definitely didn't challenge Rob, who had extra time to lie on his bed and poke fun at his brothers. To enhance self-esteem, games like these should be geared to each child's level of ability. Establishing an individual time for each child would have been more effective.

The second tactic, offering the children a story for getting dressed in time, wisely took advantage of children's interest in activities that offer a payoff. But the Gales mistakenly offered the incentive in negative terms. Rather than saying, "If you don't get ready for bed soon, there will be no story," they could have said, "Remember, we'll have a story if you get ready soon." If a follow-up was needed, they could have added, "Do you want a story? If you do, you have to get ready for bed soon." If the children still didn't respond to these more positive incentives, the parents could simply have withheld the story. The point is that positive language will have positive effects on the self-esteem of children.

Guidelines for Building Self-Esteem

- Make time demands that are appropriate for each individual child.
- Communicate expectations in advance whenever possible.
- Find ways to express expectations and incentives in a positive rather than a negative manner.

Go Fly a Kite

Charles Evans was sitting in the living room reading the evening paper when Erin, his ten-year-old daughter, interrupted his concentration. First, Erin asked him to help fix her kite. "I will after I read my newspaper," her father responded. After a moment, Erin interrupted her dad again to show him one of her math papers with a perfect score on it. Charles gave it a quick glance and returned abruptly to his paper. Finally Erin, who was growing increasingly impatient, asked her father again, "When are you going to help me fix my kite?" Charles, tired of the interruptions, ordered Erin to leave the room and stop bothering him when he was reading. The experience left them both angry and frustrated.

Reflections

Erin, young and impulsive, couldn't postpone needing her dad's attention and help. Charles contributed to the tension by letting his feelings build up until he couldn't control them, rather than expressing them earlier and asking Erin to leave the room until he was finished with the paper. He also could have set the kitchen timer and told Erin to come back for help when the buzzer went off.

Guidelines for Building Self-Esteem

- Structure the environment so that your children are not put into situations in which you lose control and act impulsively.
- Tell your children what to expect and when to expect it. Doing so will make it easier for them to wait.

"Can't You Try Harder?"

Gordy Gilbert, a shy ten-year-old, had a record of low-level work in school. His teachers found him cooperative but seemingly unconcerned about his lack of progress. During the first quarter of the school year Gordy had difficulty with English. He generally spelled words correctly, but when he included them in the sentences that his teacher dictated to the class, he made a lot of errors.

One day Gordy brought home a spelling paper with red marks all over it. At the top of the paper his teacher had written, "Gordy, so far this quarter you have made forty-one errors. Can't you try harder?"

Gordy's mother found the paper and quickly set it aside. When she and her son were alone, she calmly mentioned to Gordy that she noticed he was having a difficult time with punctuation. His resigned shrug let her know he was aware of the problem.

His mother then said, "For next week's test I want you to work especially hard on putting the correct punctuation mark at the end of each sentence. Later on we can work on capitalizing words correctly. How many sentences will be on your test?"

"Ten," Gordy said.

"OK," said his mother, "I'll give you a star for each correct punctuation mark you place at the end of a sentence. When you get ten stars, I'll take you to the zoo."

"It's a deal," said Gordy.

"Let me give you some practice sentences," said his mother. "They'll help you get ready for the test."

Reflections

Gordy's mother wisely refrained from making a big deal about the teacher's comments on Gordy's spelling paper. How could any child benefit from such a sweeping evaluation of his work and such a general admonition to "try harder"?

Doing what a good teacher would have done, Gordy's mother set a specific, manageable goal for improvement. She also challenged him by offering a reward for each correct response. As additional support, she helped him get ready for his test.

Guidelines for Building Self-Esteem

- Help your children establish specific, achievable goals for improvement and base your evaluation of their work on them.
- Rather than saying, "Can't you try harder," to motivate your children, employ attractive incentives.

"Take Your Time"

Ryan McDonald, a sensitive and open eleven-year-old, had taught his dad a lot of important things, but one of the clearest lessons came on the way home from swimming practice. Ryan had been saying that his swimming teacher, Jay, was the best teacher he had ever had. Wondering why, his father asked, "What is it about Jay as a teacher that you like so well?"

Ryan replied quickly, "He doesn't make you hurry. He says, 'Whenever you're ready to practice something, you tell me. When you're ready, then we'll begin.'"

"That's a good reason," his father responded. "We're always told to hurry up and do this and hurry up and do that. It's kind of nice to have someone say, 'Take your time; we'll start when you're ready,' isn't it?"

Ryan replied, "Yep, it sure is."

Reflections

Ryan's dad realized that children are reminded dozens of times a day—at home, at school, at play—to "hurry up." He understood that when you ask a child to hurry up, you ask him to give up his time schedule and meet someone else's. As a result, the child cannot be himself. Parents sometimes have to ask their children to hurry up, of course, but eliminating the unnecessary times will help leave their self-esteem intact.

Guidelines for Building Self-Esteem

- Reduce the need to say, "Hurry up," by building in more time (for example, by having your children get up earlier for school) and by eliminating time-consuming tasks that could be done later.
- Help schedule activities in time blocks that permit you to say, "Take your time" or "Work at your own pace."

Teens

"Perhaps We Should Let Her Fail"

The night before Tanya's first science test in seventh grade, she appeared bewildered as she randomly flipped through the pages of the chapter she was studying and glanced here and there at items on her worksheet. Unfortunately, she hadn't told her parents about the test until it was just about time for bed.

After Tanya was in bed her parents shared their concern about her lack of readiness for the test and lack of study skills. "Perhaps we should let her fail this one," her father said. "It might teach her a lesson."

"I'm not sure," responded her mother. "She seems in a pretty fragile state to me. To fail may just increase her insecurity."

After further discussion, they agreed upon an emergency plan: Tanya's father would stay up to read the chapter and then help her study in the morning.

Tanya took the test in school that day and did fairly well, thanks to her father's help.

When it was time for the next test, Tanya's parents helped her prepare for it thoroughly. Again, she did well. By the fourth test she was studying on her own and getting A's.

One day Tanya reported to her parents that the boy next to her in science class said that he wanted to study with her because he knew she was an A student.

Reflections

Tanya's parents faced a question that presents itself to all parents in a variety of situations: should we help our children or not? On the one hand, we do not want our children to become dependent on us by constantly "rescuing" them. On the other hand, we want to set them up for success by providing the proper amount of help.

Believing that Tanya lacked the skills to prepare adequately for the test, yet wanting her to begin the school year on the right foot, they wisely sacrificed their time and gave her the needed help. Had she failed, they reasoned, she could have become discouraged, and matters might have gone from bad to worse.

Helping Tanya study for the next several tests enabled her to gain the skills necessary for feeling capable. Decreasing the amount of help as she became proficient allowed her to take over responsibility for succeeding, which gave her self-confidence.

When we help our children, we want that help to foster rather than hinder their confidence in their own capabilities. Tanya's parents must have been delighted when she reported to them that a classmate had viewed her as an A student because Tanya probably began to see herself that way too.

Guidelines for Building Self-Esteem

- When you believe that your children lack the ability or willingness to succeed at a task, and when the consequences of failure have the potential of overwhelming them, go the extra mile and provide the needed help. Doing so can boost their self-esteem.

- If your children have been generally successful, if you would bet that they have the skills necessary to succeed and the personal security and stamina to bounce back from an experience of failure, and if the consequences of failure are not severe, structure the situation for long-term success by allowing them to fail, and thereby learn from their occasional mistakes.

"What Might You Say?"

Barbara Jackson and her daughter, Theresa, fourteen, had finished viewing a TV documentary on teenage pregnancy. After discussing their reactions to the program, Barbara asked, "So what would you say if you were dating a boy and he asked you to go too far sexually?"

"I'm not exactly sure what I'd say, but my answer would be no," responded Theresa.

"What might you say?" pressed Barbara.

"Well. . . ." Theresa paused.

"Would you like to try out some ways to say no?" asked her mother.

"I guess so," said Theresa.

"How about saying something like 'I don't think it's right for me to do this now'? Or," continued her mother, "'I want to wait until I'm married.' How might you say something like this in your own words?"

"Well," Theresa responded, "I could say, 'I do like you very much, but I don't feel comfortable doing this now. I want to wait.'"

"That's a good response," said her mother. "Knowing what you're going to say will make it so much easier for you to handle this kind of situation."

Reflections

Barbara apparently recognized that Theresa needed some help in responding wisely to an invitation to become involved sexually. Talking through a hypothetical situation not only helped Theresa know what to say if the situation arose, but also gave her a chance to try out a response. We need to prepare our children for the difficult situations they may face involving sex, drugs, cheating in school, dealing with loss, and other social concerns. Doing so, without preaching to them, will help structure a potential situation for success and thus contribute to their feelings of self-worth.

Guidelines for Building Self-Esteem

- Prepare your children and youth for situations that may catch them off guard by inviting them to practice various responses they could make. Doing so will help them be successful, which will give them added self-confidence.

"I Did Pretty Good and I Had a Great Time"

Fourteen-year-old Teri Denesen was preparing to try out for a local children's theater production, and she encouraged her thirteen-year-old brother, Mark, to try out as a dancer because she knew he would enjoy the experience. Their mother, overhearing this, was flabbergasted, since she knew that Mark was not exactly the epitome of grace. Yet he told his sister that he would love to come and try out. He thought he had "good rhythm"; he was eager to go!

Their mother kept quiet and drove them to the tryouts, where twenty young boys faced the music. Mark was not among the best, but he wasn't among the worst either. He greeted the news that he was not chosen with a sigh and then a grin. "I knew that I wasn't the best," he said. "But I did pretty good and I had a great time."

"I was proud of you," his mother said.

Reflections

Mark's sister suggested that he go to the tryout because she felt he'd enjoy the experience. She may not have been thinking much about whether he'd get a part. And, in fact, Mark had a wonderful time. Fortunately, his mother realized that she'd almost prevented it by assuming that the experience would be worthless unless Mark had a chance to win.

Guidelines for Building Self-Esteem

- Do not make all the decisions about what experiences will or will not be valuable for your children.
- Understand that your children don't mind "losing" if they enjoy the process. They may not view failure the same way adults do.
- Do not evaluate your children by adult standards. Too many children feel they must live up to overexacting adult expectations.

"I Know I'm Late"

Before sixteen-year-old Eric left for the homecoming dance, his father reminded him of their agreement: "Remember you agreed that you will be home by midnight. If you get home on time, you can continue using the car. If you don't, you will not be allowed to use it for two weeks. If there is an emergency, like a flat tire, remember to call. Now, tell me in your own words what our agreement is."

"OK, Dad—I'll be home by midnight or lose my car privileges for two weeks," responded Eric.

At 12:45 Eric arrived home. He slipped into his parent's bedroom and left a note that read, "Dear Mom and Dad, I had a great time. I know I'm late. I will take the consequences. Love, Eric."

The next morning, Eric's father greeted him by asking about the homecoming dance. After listening to his son's account, he said, "Thanks for your note, Eric. We're glad you had a good time and that you got home safely. You didn't meet the 12:00 deadline, however, so we're going to have to uphold our agreement. I hope that not using the car for the next two weeks will help remind you to be on time."

Reflections

Eric's father wisely established a contract with him prior to his leaving for the homecoming dance. Reminding Eric of this agreement helped to reduce the power struggle that could have developed when he arrived home late and received the consequences.

Asking Eric about the dance prior to administering the consequences expressed personal interest in him. Saying that he was glad Eric had a good time and had arrived home safely expressed personal concern. Both communications likely increased Eric's feelings of self-worth.

His father's statement, "I hope that not using the car for the next two weeks will help remind you to be on time," was very positive. It implied that the consequence was intended to be constructive and that Eric would be allowed to use the car again in the future.

Guidelines for Building Self-Esteem

- Decrease self-defeating power struggles with your children by establishing contracts that specify expectations and consequences.
- Encourage understanding and ownership of agreements you make with your children by having them restate them in their own words.
- Administer consequences to children in a way that communicates you are being constructive rather than punitive.

Communication Skills for Structuring for Feelings of Success

Following are the most critical verbal communication skills for carrying out the structuring principle. Also included are examples of what you *might* say in carrying out each skill.

- **Communicate expectations to your children specifically and positively.** For example:

  Don't say: (generally) I want you to be home early tonight.
  Say: (specifically) I want you to be in the house by 10:00.

  Don't say: (Negatively) Don't eat your green beans with your spoon.
  Say: (Positively) Please use your fork to eat your green beans.

- **Check your child's understanding of the expectation.** For example:

  Say: Tell me in your own words what I have asked you to do.
  Say: What is your understanding of our agreement?

- **Offer reasons for your expectations.** For example:

  Say: I don't want you to ride your bike to Aaron's because it's getting dark and you don't have a light.
  Say: I want you to get your homework finished now because we're going shopping after dinner.

- **State your expectations in advance.** For example:

Say: Tomorrow after school I want you to mow the lawn.

Say: When your program is over, I want you to go to bed.

- **Clarify your expectations.** For example:

  Say: (Specifically) Meet me at the ball park, the one next to your school, not the one by the post office.

  Say: (Showing a good example and a bad example) Pick out some ripe peaches like this one, not like the one over there.

  Say: (Summarizing) Remember now, we have agreed on two things: You will be home by 11:00, and you will call if there is an emergency.

- **Establish incentives.** For example:

  Don't say: (Generally) When you pick up your toys, we'll do something fun.

  Say: (Specifically) When you pick up your toys, I'll read you the story about Curious George.

  Don't say: (Negatively) If you don't take a bite of everything, you can't have dessert.

  Say: (Positively) When you take a bite of everything, you can have dessert.

  Say: (Being open to the child's interests) What would you like to do that's special when your homework is finished?

- **Offer help.** For example:

  Say: Do you want me to help you, or do you want to do it yourself?

  Say: How can I be helpful?

Developmental Needs of Children to Be Considered When Structuring for Feelings of Success

Younger, less mature children need:

- specific directions and examples of what is expected.
- expectations that are limited in scope and not very complicated.
- tangible, immediate rewards.
- considerable help made available to them.
- environments that are structured but permit freedom within defined limits.
- evaluations of performance that consider their limited ability and experience.

Older, more mature children need:

- expectations that are more complex.
- less tangible incentives and more deferred rewards.
- help when they ask for it.
- less-structured environments.
- evaluations of performance that consider their greater ability and experience.

Summary

W e have stressed in this chapter the importance of structuring situations to help children experience feelings of success rather than failure. Here are the basic guidelines that we emphasized:

1. Set appropriate expectations—don't expect adult behavior from your children.

2. Clearly communicate your expectations in terms your children can understand.

3. Provide attractive incentives for your children.

4. Offer the right amount of help—when in doubt, ask your children.

5. Remove obstacles in the environment that cause your children to fail. Build in supports that will help them succeed.

6. Provide reasonable evaluations—do not judge your children according to adult standards.

The principle outlined in this chapter assumes that we'll want our children to look good rather than bad and have feelings of success rather than failure. It is just not true that children will thrive in the long run if repeatedly confronted with criticism, lots of prescriptions, and failure. We need to help our children succeed from their perspective as well as ours.

We do not mean to imply that we should never permit our children to fail. In fact, children should know that it is OK to fail. But while failure can be constructive, an overall pattern of success will have the greatest positive effect on self-esteem.

Let's not only catch our children being successful, let's set them up for success.

Principle Three

Give Your Children a Feeling of Reasonable Control over Their Lives

To have self-esteem, children must feel they have some degree of control over their lives. They need to feel that they can make some decisions about such matters as what to wear, where to go, what to do, and what to say. And they must feel that they can generally control what belongs to them. When children are overcontrolled they will not feel very confident and capable.

Children can also suffer from low self-esteem when parents exercise too little control. When they do not exert enough control, their children will grow up feeling unprepared for life and neglected. The result will be low self-esteem.

Children need an amount of control over their lives that is consistent with their level of maturity. We call this "reasonable control."

You probably know overcontrolling parents who respond this way to their children:

Child: Can I mow the lawn?
Parent: No, you're too small.

Child: I'd like to stay overnight at Mary's house.
Parent: No, you can't leave your sister here all alone.

Child: I want to wear the red shirt.
Parent: No, the green one is just fine.

Child: I can't do anything I want to do.
Parent: Stop complaining or go to your room.

It's easy to say, "No you can't." But children who live in a prison of "noes" tend to have less self-confidence and self-respect.

Since what constitutes over- and undercontrol will depend on the personalities of your children and their stage of development, it is important to listen to them. They'll let you know when you should back off and when you should get more involved. Recently, a parent we know was helping his twelve-year-old son start the mower to cut the neighbor's lawn for the first time. After the mower was started, his son looked him directly in the eye and said, "You can go home now." We must continually watch for indications that our children are able to control their lives or are frustrated by too much parental control. Then we should respond accordingly.

The following short accounts illustrate the principle of allowing reasonable control.

Early Childhood

"I'm Going to Hold Her"

Jan and Ken Lancaster were proud of their new baby, Melissa, and anxious to do everything right. They studied books to find out how often to feed babies and how much babies should sleep. They generally tried to keep to a schedule, and Melissa seemed to thrive.

One evening, they put the baby to bed and began to play bridge with friends. Suddenly Melissa began to cry. They checked carefully, but she was neither hungry nor wet nor seemingly in great pain. They went back to the bridge table, but the cries continued.

After a few minutes Ken said, "She doesn't cry like this often. I'm sorry to break the game, but I'm going to hold her until she goes back to sleep. I'm not comfortable hearing her scream."

"I think that's a good idea," said Jan.

Reflections

By being responsive to Melissa's cries, Jan and Ken helped her to feel some degree of control over them. Consistent, responsive care helps infants develop a generalized sense of being able to affect their environment. Lack of such care leads them to doubt their ability to influence their environment and, in turn, to feel incapable.

While children, as they grow up, need to be taught that they cannot always have their own way, infants need to feel they have the ability to affect their environment. Jan and Ken played their cards right when they decided to hold their baby.

Guidelines for Building Self-Esteem

- Allow infants to have a feeling of reasonable control over their lives by providing consistent, responsive care. Such care will lay a strong foundation for self-esteem.

"Wow, Am I Strong"

Connie Laski, a single parent, career woman, and all-around "super mom" loved to spend as much time as she could with her two-year-old, Sher. One of their favorite playtime activities was to wrestle and tumble on the soft carpet. Sher appeared especially pleased with herself when she would push on her mother and her mother would fall over. Sher's response seemed to say, "Wow, am I strong!"

Reflections

Sher's mother probably knew that it made her daughter feel in control when she rolled over in response to her shove. Even though it wasn't "actual" control, Sher experienced feelings of being able to influence her environment.

Guidelines for Building Self-Esteem

- Give small children opportunities to feel that they can influence objects and events by building in supports and responses that make them feel that they are in control.

"I Want to Stay Small"

Four-year-old Jimmy Olson, a determined type, consistently wouldn't eat his supper. His parents had tried various strategies to get him to eat. One time they told him, "You're going to have to eat if you want to grow." His response was, "I want to stay small." Other strategies found

Jimmy sitting at the table long after the rest of the family had finished, refusing to eat the required two bites of everything.

One evening, after a number of unsuccessful meals with Jimmy, his parents decided not to put any food on his plate. When Jimmy questioned his empty plate, his father matter-of-factly reassured him that they wanted to include him at the table but since he hadn't been eating his supper, they didn't want to waste food. When Jimmy cried, "But I want dessert!" his mother gently reminded him that family members had to eat at least two bites of each portion of food on their plates before they got dessert or could be excused from the table.

After Jimmy had complained for a few minutes, his mother invited him to help determine what amount of food would constitute two bites. Gradually he bought into this scheme and cleaned his plate without much comment. The next night, they repeated the same strategy, and again Jimmy finished a reasonable portion of food without a hassle.

Reflections

How parents handle meals with their children can have a great effect on their self-esteem. Telling Jimmy that he would have to eat to grow wasn't very meaningful to him at his stage of development, since four-year-olds cannot think much about the value of being a grown-up. Forcing a determined, self-centered four-year-old to sit at the table until he took two bites of everything only heightened the tension. But giving him some control over how much he had to eat motivated him to finish his meal. Allowing him to participate in the decision probably made him feel capable and increased his self-esteem.

Guidelines for Building Self-Esteem

- Involve children in helping to establish expectations for themselves.
- Let children negotiate with you to some degree. Doing so will help them feel they have some control over their lives.
- Don't let mealtime become a power struggle between you and your children.

Snack Here, Not There

One day, absorbed in their five-year-old world, Andrea and her friend Jenny inadvertently wandered into the family room with their peanut butter sandwiches. Noticing this, Andrea's mother called her to the kitchen and said, "Remember, we always eat our food in the kitchen. Please bring your sandwiches in here now."

In response, Andrea called to Jenny, "Come here in the kitchen. Let's eat our sandwiches at the snack table."

Reflections

In correcting Andrea's behavior, her mother avoided a potential power struggle by appealing to a rule that had been clearly established. Being able to refer to the rule helped remove Andrea's mother as the adversary. If there was an adversary, it was the rule. For most children under the age of seven, referring to rules is an effective way of guiding their behavior.

Reminding Andrea privately was a sensitive thing to do. It helped Andrea's mother establish herself as a friend interested in helping her avoid problems.

Guidelines for Building Self-Esteem

- For children who are six or seven years old or younger, appealing to a rule is an effective means of guiding or correcting their behavior.
- When possible, confront infractions of a rule privately. Avoiding unnecessary embarrassment will protect the self-esteem of young children.

Middle Childhood

Choices

Jean Smith was taking her two children, ages six and seven, to the grocery store. On the way there, she told them they could each help pick out a few items. She thought that by letting them make some selections, they could make use of what they'd recently learned in school about the four food groups. She also thought that if her children were given a chance to help buy groceries, they'd feel more capable and confident.

As they headed down the first aisle, Jean reminded them that they had to choose a nutritious cereal and that, while she would accept their selections, she reserved the right to make the final decision if they could not agree on a purchase.

Later, when the girls got into a dispute about what cereal to buy, Jean said, "Do you want to decide together which cereal to buy or should one of you choose the cereal and the other the fruit?"

The girls agreed to make individual choices and Jean thanked them for helping to solve the problem.

Reflections

Mrs. Smith apparently realized the value of giving her children the opportunity to make reasonable choices. Quite often when children experience problems of working together, parents too quickly solve the problem for them. In this account, Jean involved her children further in solving their own problem by having them decide how to decide.

Guidelines for Building Self-Esteem

- Give your children the opportunity to learn how to make decisions so they'll know that you have confidence in them. When your children see that you respect them for their decisions, they'll begin to see themselves as worthy of respect.
- Clearly define the limits of choice so that your children know what alternatives are available.
- Support their choices. Reward and praise your children for their ability to make a choice, even though you might have made a different one.

"But He's My Friend, Mom"

Seven-year-old Alex Jordan came home from school very excited. He had recently made a new friend, Brendan, who had asked him to stay overnight at his house on Friday. Alex's mother hesitated, however. "I don't feel comfortable letting you stay with people I don't know," she said.

"But he's my friend, Mom."

"You like him a lot and really want to go, don't you?" she responded.

"Yes," replied Alex.

"I'm not going to make any promises," said his mother, "but let me talk to some parents who know Brendan's family, and if they think it's OK for you to stay overnight at his house, I'll call his mother and see if it'll be all right. I'll try my best to make this happen."

Reflections

Alex's mother could have handled this situation in many ways, but the important thing she did was to let Alex know that she was on his side and would make an effort to support his interests. If, after exhausting all options, she concluded that it was unwise to let Alex go, he would know that at least she'd made an effort to accommodate him.

Guidelines for Building Self-Esteem

- Recognize the natural tendency to protect your children, and avoid being overprotective.
- When children ask to do something, begin with the attitude, "Why not?" rather than, "Why?"

"It's My Money"

Every week when he was in third grade, Jon Harper got an allowance, which he regularly spent on a collection of stickers bought at the local grocery store. Collecting these stickers was the "in" thing to do at his school.

Realizing what his hobby was costing, his mother said, "Jon, you've spent almost ten dollars on those silly stickers. That's enough. It's such a waste of money."

Jon responded, "But, Mom, we're having a contest to see who can get the whole series first. Please, you said that I could spend up to ten dollars of my own money any way I wanted to, and this is how I want to spend it."

Thinking it over, his mother said, "Yes, I can see it's important to you, and it is your money. Go ahead if you want to."

Reflections

Jon's mother thought that spending ten dollars on stickers was foolish. Jon did not. For the sake of Jon's self-esteem, she wisely allowed him to go along with the crowd and make a decision that she felt wasn't very sensible.

Guidelines for Building Self-Esteem

- Allow your children to control some amount of money, however small. Doing so will help them make choices and give them some control over their lives.
- Accept your children's choices in areas where you have given them control, even when you feel they're not the best choices.

"Let Me Do It, Dad"

Joe Kramer, age nine, and his father were building a racer for the Cub Scout pinewood derby. The rules for the contest stated that the child had to complete the project, with a parent supervising and occasionally helping out.

Joe was dextrous and creative, but his father took most of the initiative in planning and building the racer. It was Joe's father who suggested that they design it like a Corvette, and despite an occasional, "Let me do it, Dad," it was Joe's father who manned the coping saw as the block of wood became a car. Joe did a little of the sanding, but his father put the finishing touches on to make sure it was "right." When the racer was complete, it indeed looked just like a Corvette, and Joe won the prize for the best-designed car.

Reflections

Perhaps Joe's father did much of the work on the car because he wanted Joe to enjoy the fruits of winning. Maybe he was caught up in the competition with other fathers. Regardless of the reason, the result was that Joe did not get either to use his abilities or to develop them further. More than likely, Joe got from his father the implicit message that he was not big enough or good enough to do what the Cub Scout program thought he could. While Joe received some recognition for designing the best racer, he probably wasn't as proud as he would have been if he'd been more responsible for the final product.

Guidelines for Building Self-Esteem

- Give your children some feeling of control at various stages of a joint venture. In doing so, you'll reinforce them as capable.
- If in doubt about whether to help your children, ask them if they would like your help.
- Try to help your children by eliciting their ideas rather than imposing your own.

Puzzled

One evening nine-year-old Stephen and his mother began a jigsaw puzzle on the card table in the family room. Unfortunately, there wasn't enough time to complete the puzzle, so Stephen's mother had to say, "I'm sorry, Stephen, but we'll have to finish this tomorrow. It's time for bed."

"But I want to do it now!" Stephen whined. "It won't take long."

"I wish we could," his mother said. "But there isn't enough time. We'll finish it tomorrow. Do you want to put it in the living room or in your bedroom?"

"In my bedroom," Stephen responded reluctantly.

Reflections

Stephen's mother wisely avoided a prolonged power struggle by having him focus on the choice of where to put the puzzle rather than on the issue of continuing or not continuing to do the puzzle.

While Stephen may have been unhappy about stopping the project, he must have felt some degree of control when his mother asked him where he wanted to have the puzzle kept.

Guidelines for Building Self-Esteem

- Avoid prolonged power struggles with your children over some object, activity, or issue by refocusing their attention on something else.

- Look for ways of giving your children choices, even in situations in which you have to set limits on their behavior.
- Express understanding of and empathy toward your children's feelings when you cannot accommodate their wishes.

"They'll Laugh at Me"

Ahmad, age ten, and his dad were arriving at the school parking lot one Sunday, the day all of the Little League soccer teams were meeting to bus to a professional soccer game. Rain had been forecast for the entire day, and it was beginning to rain as they parked the car.

As Ahmad looked at the kids and coaches milling around the parking lot, he noticed that he was the only one wearing a yellow raincoat. "I'm not going to wear this raincoat," he told his father. "No one else has a raincoat on. I'd look silly."

"Would you rather look silly or get pneumonia?" his father asked.

"But, Dad, the kids will laugh at me. They'll call me a sissy."

"Don't worry about what other kids say," his dad responded. "You'll be the only warm and dry kid if it rains."

Finally, Ahmad, seeing a jacket of his in the rear window of the car, begged his dad, "Please, can I wear this jacket instead?"

Reluctantly, his father agreed, "Oh, I suppose so, but you'll be sorry. I swear, you're getting more childish everyday."

Reflections

Most of us have experienced this kind of conflict with our children. Ahmad's father wanted his son to keep warm and dry so he'd enjoy the soccer game and stay healthy. Ahmad was more concerned about fitting in with other kids. Allowing Ahmad to dress like his peers probably helped his self-esteem, but his father's parting comment about being childish was unreasonable.

Guidelines for Building Self-Esteem

- Provide reasonable opportunities for your children to conform to their peer group. This does not mean they should be allowed to conform all the time, but at least when consequences are not major.
- Do not put your children down when they express a desire to be like their peers. Strange as it may seem, if you accept this desire, your children will likely become less defensive about yielding to peer pressure, and that may help move them beyond the need for peer approval.

"We Did It Ourselves!"

On the Saturday before Easter, Anne Wells would always make cakes in the shape of Easter Bunnies for the neighbors. In the past, her children, Todd and Mary, age ten and twelve, had watched with interest. Now they said they were ready to make the cakes themselves.

"Please, Mom. We know how to do it. You just relax."

"Well, OK, I'll just be the overseer," said Anne.

As the baking began, Anne found she couldn't hold back; she cautioned against spilling, volunteered to break the eggs, and offered to color the coconut.

"Mom, we can do it! We want to do it our way. We'll clean the kitchen when we're finished."

Realizing that she could not keep herself from meddling, Anne got a book and retired to the living room. Two hours later she was ushered into the kitchen where the cakes were displayed. They were not exactly like hers, but she was surprised at what an excellent job the kids had done. The kids took them to the neighbors and proudly announced, "We made them this year! We did it ourselves!"

Reflections

Anne knew that her children wanted very much to complete the project on their own, so she wisely left the scene when she realized she couldn't help interfering. The experience seemed rewarding to them, and it represented another significant step toward managing their own affairs.

Guidelines for Building Self-Esteem

- Allow your children some opportunities to work according to their own standards. They would often rather have the freedom to make mistakes on their own than end up with a product that's perfect from an adult's point of view.
- Resist the temptation to overadvise children on projects that you've allowed or asked them to do. When you see your children attempt a task you've done many times, you may feel compelled to tell them the best, fastest, neatest, easiest way. Leave the area if the temptation to do this is too strong.

"What Should I Wear?"

 inona Banks, age ten, was getting ready to go shopping with her mother. Pausing at the bedroom door, she said, "Mom, what shall I wear?"

Her mother replied, "Honey, you can wear anything you want to. You're old enough to make those decisions by yourself."

Winona went into the bedroom and got dressed. When she came out, her mother looked at her and exclaimed, "You can't wear red socks with a purple skirt!"

"But you told me I could wear anything I wanted to," protested Winona. "I think it looks nice."

"Well, within reason," her mother said. "Now go put on white socks."

Reflections

Winona's mother created a problem for her daughter by first giving her control over what to wear and then taking it away from her. If Winona's mother couldn't tolerate any choice, she should have set some guidelines for her daughter or laid out several outfits for her to choose from. By rejecting Winona's choice, she probably made her feel that *she* had been rejected. A pattern of such rejections could only hurt Winona's self-confidence and make her reluctant to make future decisions on her own.

Guidelines for Building Self-Esteem

- Accept the decisions you've allowed your children to make.
- Avoid ridicule and sarcasm when reacting to decisions your children have made.

"All My Friends Are Going To"

Robert Gregory, an ambitious ten-year-old, was beginning to feel a strong need for peer approval. It was increasingly important that he do what his friends did. One evening, he asked his mother and father if he could play Little League hockey. "All my friends are going to," he said.

"I'm afraid not. It's too dangerous," said his mother to her disappointed son.

His father added, "You'd be one of the smallest boys on the team, and we couldn't bear to have you injured. We can't let you play."

But the Gregorys' response satisfied neither their son nor themselves; they all felt frustrated. They knew it was important for Robert to play hockey, yet they strongly believed there were reasons why he shouldn't. Since they wanted to give Robert a chance to develop his talents, they called the Little League director to get more information about the program. The director assured them that coaches were extremely safety-conscious and allowed no roughhousing, so injuries were rare. Reassured, the Gregorys changed their minds and let Robert play hockey with his friends.

Reflections

Robert's parents faced a classic problem of control. They sensed how important it was to let Robert play hockey for the sake of his own development, yet their first concern was to protect him from injury. Getting an outside view helped them make their decision.

Guidelines for Building Self-Esteem

- If possible, allow your children to join in with friends on various activities. They need to feel included in a group.
- After carefully considering the facts, be willing to take some risks in permitting your children to do things that will increase their self-confidence.

"I Guess You Were Right"

Mike Moreno was a likeable, adventuresome twelve-year-old who generally demonstrated good judgment. One day, he begged his parents to let him have a paper route. His parents hesitated, knowing that he already played softball and took piano lessons, but Mike assured them he could handle it. When they finally consented, they told him they expected him to keep the route for at least a year.

For six months, Mike faithfully and conscientiously executed the duties of the paper route. It soon became apparent, however, that he was burning the candle at both ends, and it was too exhausting for him. Mike finally had to admit to his parents, "I guess you were right after all. This paper route is just too much for me. I'm tired all the time. Could I possibly quit, even though my year isn't up?"

His father said, "Yes, I think that would be wise. You've done a good job, and I'm glad you wanted to give it a try. Maybe later on, when you have more free time, you can try a paper route again."

Reflections

Mike had a wise father, who knew that a child's judgment may not be the best in the long run. Mike had learned by experience that he couldn't handle the paper route, but his father didn't make him "stick to his guns no matter what" to try to build his character. Knowing when to stick to your guns and when to be flexible is the important thing.

Mike's dad didn't say, "I told you so," either, or force Mike to continue the route as punishment for the "poor" judgment he showed in wanting to try it in the first place. Mike learned that it's OK to make a mistake and that his parents trusted him enough to allow him to help shape his own circumstances.

Guidelines for Building Self-Esteem

- Allow your children to make some errors in judgment and learn from their mistakes. Do not make them "pay" psychologically or physically when their decisions, in fact, turn out to be unwise.
- Help your children think through the advantages and disadvantages of decisions they make.

Teens

"I Don't Care What the Other Kids Do"

Although she was unique in many ways, Shannon Gallagher was a typical fourteen-year-old in that she wanted to be accepted by her peer group. She needed to belong. As she got ready to leave for school one morning, her mother noticed a comb sticking out of the back pocket of her jeans. "That comb looks ridiculous," said her mother. "Why don't you put it in your purse where it belongs?"

"Mother, all the kids put their combs in their back pockets," replied Shannon. "Every single kid in my group keeps a comb there, and that's where I want to keep mine."

"Well, I don't care what the other kids do. It looks sloppy and you're not going to do it. Now take that comb out of your pocket and put it in your purse."

Shannon glared at her mother, jammed the comb in her purse, and left for school. When she was safely out of her mother's sight, she stuck the comb back in her pocket.

Reflections

During early adolescence, children who have been anxious to please their parents often transfer this desire to their peer group. What seems insignificant to a parent may seem like a matter of life or death to an adolescent. Parents who try to maintain their authority in such cases may encourage their children to deceive them, since children don't want to stand out as odd in the eyes of their peers. Shannon's mother should probably have allowed her to carry her comb where all her friends carried theirs.

Guidelines for Building Self-Esteem

- Allow your adolescent to "go along with the crowd" in a variety of small ways. It's important that they know they can be trusted to control certain aspects of their lives.
- Allow the will of your children to prevail when the stakes are small. Doing so fosters a spirit of cooperation between them and you. Then, when you need to exert your authority in important situations, your children will be much more likely to view you as fair and to cooperate.

"Hang Up Your Jacket"

The mother of fifteen-year-old Tim arrived home a bit tired from working all day. As she entered the house, she noticed a familiar jacket in a familiar place: on the floor in the hallway. At that moment Tim appeared. "Tim, hang up your jacket! When I get home from a hard day, I don't want to see a messy house."

Reflections

Tim's mother had reason to be disappointed. She probably had worked hard all day and would have welcomed some help from him. But for the sake of Tim's self-esteem, she might have first offered a greeting and inquired about his day before bringing up the issue of the jacket. Her haste to control Tim's behavior sent him the message that a tidy house was more important to her than he was.

Guidelines for Building Self-Esteem

- When meeting or leaving your children, show support and affection and steer clear of advice and reprimands. Such consideration tells them that they are valued and worthy of esteem.
- When exercising control over your children, do so in a way that leaves their self-esteem intact.

"But, Dad . . ."

One evening soon after dinner, seventeen-year-old Todd put on his coat and headed toward the door. I'm going over to Sarah's," he said.

"Oh no you're not," his father responded. "Not until you get permission. You can't just go anywhere you want, anytime you want."

"But, Dad, we have plans."

"I don't care what plans you have. You're not going to leave this house anytime you feel like it. You're still part of this family and under my authority until you're eighteen."

"But, Dad . . ."

Reflections

Todd apparently thought he was old enough to make this type of decision for himself. His father did not. Differences such as this lead to major power struggles between parents and teenagers.

While we cannot let teenagers do anything they want anytime they want to do it, it is important to realize that they naturally spread their wings for independent flight. We ought to be concerned if they don't.

To have avoided the power struggle that developed and maintained Todd's sense of self-worth, his father could have said, "I get upset when you make your own plans without checking with us." This message would have invited Todd to respond to a problem that his father was experiencing. Todd's father may also have avoided the power struggle by asking Todd at the dinner table what he planned to do that night.

Guidelines for Building Self-Esteem

- Realize that it is natural for teenagers to move toward independence. Communicate with them in a way that respects and even rewards progress they make toward self-control.
- Rather than always exerting your authority when your children do something you don't like, express how you feel about their behavior. For example, say, "I get irritated when you track mud into the house because it makes extra work for me." Doing so will give them an opportunity to change their behavior on their own.

Communication Skills for Allowing Reasonable Control

Following are some of the more important skills for giving your children feelings of increased control over their lives. The degree to which you allow your children to make decisions is, of course, dependent on their age and maturity level.

- **Offer choices.** For example:

  Don't say: Put on your green dress.
  Say: You can wear the green, red, or yellow dress. You may choose.

- **Communicate acceptance of some part of a child's request even when you cannot accommodate the entire request.** For example:

  Don't say: No, Adam can't sleep over tonight. We have too many things to do.
  Say: Adam can't stay overnight because we are leaving for Grandma's early in the morning. You *can* have him come over to play after school.

- **Use "I" rather than "You" messages.** ("I" messages invite children to respond to *your* concern.) For example:

  Don't say: (You) Stop slamming the door.
  Say: I feel angry (feeling) when you slam the door (behavior) because I can't concentrate on my work (reason for the feeling).

- **State preferences rather than demands.** For example:

  Don't say: You are absolutely not going to that movie.
  Say: I would prefer that you don't go to the movie, but you can make the decision for yourself.

- **Tell what can be done when you tell what can't be done.** For example:

  Say: You can't go into the dining room because we have our income tax material on the table. You can go in there when we are finished on Saturday.

Say: You can't go swimming now. You can this coming Friday.

- **Allow for negotiation.** For example:

Don't say: I don't want to talk about it.
Say: Let's talk about it and see if together we can come up with a reasonable plan.

Developmental Needs of Children That Should Be Considered in Applying the Control Skills

Younger, less mature children need:

- concrete, simple, and specific statements of the boundaries within which their decisions can be made.
- opportunities to make some impulsive decisions.
- opportunities to make decisions that are self-serving.
- concrete, immediate reinforcement of their efforts and accomplishments in making decisions and managing their own lives.

Older, more mature children need:

- more opportunity to control their own time.
- opportunities to think through, evaluate, and learn from the consequences of their decisions.
- opportunities to make decisions acceptable to their peer group.

Summary

C hildren naturally want some degree of control over their lives. When we overcontrol them we communicate that they are incapable and that they should fear the world. When we undercontrol them, however, we communicate that they are insignificant and unloved. Both over- and undercontrol can damage their self-esteem. Giving our children opportunities to exercise reasonable control over their own affairs will stimulate them to feel capable and confident; providing reasonable limits to self-control will let them know we care about them.

The principle offered in this chapter encourages us to cultivate an attitude of "Why not" rather than "Why" when our children ask to do something. If we discover that they are not ready to do it, we should ask ourselves how we can help them get ready. We need to direct our efforts at helping our children get control of their lives.

Giving our children opportunities to think through their problems and make many of their own decisions will help build their self-confidence.

Reinforce Your Children as Lovable and Capable

uman behavior tends to remain in effect if it is re-warded. If a child is reinforced (praised and rewarded) for completing his homework on time, he'll tend to keep on completing it on time. Reinforcing our children as lovable and capable is one way of helping them feel good about themselves. When we praise and reward them for who they are and what they can do, they will tend to feel lovable and capable. In other words, their self-esteem will tend to be high.

Helping Our Children Feel Lovable

The most obvious way to help our children feel lovable is to tell them they are loved. We know a family with young boys that concludes its bedtime prayers with the petition, "Watch and guard the boys through the night and keep them safe 'til morning light because we love them very much, and we know that You do too." After the prayer, the parents kiss each child goodnight and say something like, "I love you."

In addition to verbal expressions, we can demonstrate our love in ways that may be even more effective for some children. Most young children appreciate physical expressions of love such as touching and hugging. While physical expressions may be difficult for some people, they boost children's self-esteem in powerful ways.

One cautionary note: We need to be careful that our expressions of love to our children do not depend on their competence. Unconditional love provides the real basis for personal security and self-esteem. Every once in a while, we should let our children know that we would love them even if they were not so competent. "I really like to see you so well organized," you might say. "But you know something? I'd love you even if you weren't."

Helping Our Children Feel Capable

We help our children feel capable as well as lovable by helping them feel confident about doing things at home, performing what is expected in school, joining in with friends in various social activities, expressing themselves to others, trying new things, and solving problems. Self-confidence about what they can do is basic to children's self-esteem.

When we were in a restaurant working on this book, one of us encountered a little boy in the restroom who had high regard for his capabilities. The conversation went something like this:

"Are you in this restroom all by yourself?" the man asked.

"Yes, I'm a big boy."

"You must be a big boy if you can come in here all by yourself."

"I've got a Mickey Mouse watch," the boy replied.

"You have your own Mickey Mouse watch?"

"Yeah, and I can tell time, too."

"Wow," the man said. "You must be a big boy if you can tell time."

"I know everything in the whole universe," the boy declared.

This little boy not only felt confident talking to any adult, he also felt good about what he knew and what he could do.

Fundamental to helping our children feel capable is fostering within them an "I-can-do-it" attitude. We can generate this attitude in a variety of ways: by trusting them to move on to new challenges, by telling them that they "can do it," by liberally praising them for their accomplishments, and by helping them think and talk positively about themselves. Positive mental attitude is not just a gimmick. It is an avenue to competence and positive self-regard.

Early Childhood

"Good for You, Carolyn!"

Two-year-old Carolyn Vang was playing with her toys one day when she suddenly started to pick them up and put them back in the toy chest. Her mother, who had been watching, clapped with delight and said, "Good for you, Carolyn! You're putting your toys away." Carolyn looked up in amazement and then immediately began putting more toys in the chest. Her mother again applauded enthusiastically.

Reflections

It's never too early to reinforce behavior that you would like to see in your children. Although Carolyn was too young to pick her toys up regularly, when she did happen to pick them up, her mother took advantage of the opportunity by reinforcing the behavior with praise and applause.

Guidelines for Building Self-Esteem

- Reinforce behaviors in your children that you want to see repeated, even when they happen unintentionally. Clapping is an excellent way to reinforce younger children.
- Emphasize the positive with young children. If you spend too much time pointing out what your young children do wrong, they may grow up feeling that's the only way to get attention.

Sing Me a Song

During opening exercises at Sunday School, five-year-old Bruce was asked by the song leader if he would come to the front and join him in singing a song they had learned during their Wednesday evening youth program. Bruce responded to the invitation by leaning toward his mother, clutching her arm, and shaking his head no.

Immediately realizing that Bruce did not feel secure enough to do the duet with him, the song leader said, "That's OK. Maybe we can do it sometime later when there are other children to join you."

His mother responded, "I'll give him an opportunity to sing it for me at home this afternoon."

After Sunday School was over the song leader knelt down so he was at Bruce's level, put his arm around his shoulder, and after talking with him a bit said, "It was OK that you didn't sing in Sunday School today. We will get some of the other kids in our Wednesday group to practice the song with you, and maybe you can all come to the front and sing it sometime. Would you like to do that, Bruce?"

Bruce shook his head yes.

Reflections

We need to read carefully our children's willingness and ability to perform for others. There is no greater feeling of personal destruction than to be asked in front of others to perform for them when you don't feel comfortable doing so.

The song leader wisely backed off and reinforced Bruce as OK even though he didn't perform. Bruce's mother also provided needed support by saying that she would invite him to sing it for her at home.

Talking personally with Bruce after Sunday School was over helped communicate that he was still loved.

Guidelines for Building Self-Esteem

- Reinforce your children as lovable in situations in which their lack of personal security has made them unwilling to perform publicly.
- Initiate a conversation with your children after they have experienced an uncomfortable situation as a way of showing them they are still loved.

Middle Childhood

"Show 'Em, Kelly!"

The Merritt's had long known the importance of demonstrating warmth and respect for their children, Kelly, six, and Glenn, eight. They had, for example, made a practice of displaying the children's drawings and paintings on the refrigerator door, posting certificates of completion from swimming classes and other sporting events in their rooms, and putting up their photographs around the house. They were also generous with verbal and physical praise.

The Merritts made a special attempt to praise Kelly and Glenn publicly. When it was necessary, they reprimanded Kelly and Glenn, but they always tried to do this in private. When their friends were over, the Merritts could be heard to say, "Nice job on your math today" or "Glenn scored a goal in the Mite's hockey game yesterday" or "Kelly is good at making friends."

The parents also created opportunites for their children to "show off," not arrogantly, but in a way that would demonstrate their pride. "Watch Kelly skate," they would say. "Show 'em, Kelly!"

Reflections

The public dimension of praise or reprimand is important. Publicly praising a child by displaying her drawings and homework or creating opportunities for her to show off her abilities boosts self-esteem and communicates to her that she is not only capable but loved, respected, and admired. In the same way, rejecting a child's behavior in public, even with only one other child present, adds to the embarrassment of the moment. While you cannot always avoid doing so, it is preferable to remove a child to a private setting when you administer a reprimand. Doing so has important consequences. Your child will learn that you still respect him, which will serve to prevent a further hassle, for it is often to "save face" that a child will continue antagonizing an adult who is reprimanding him.

Guidelines for Building Self-Esteem

- Reinforce your children for demonstrating their talents and abilities.

- Praise your children in public as well as in private. Whenever possible, reprimand your children in private.

"You Have a Lot of Good Ideas"

When six-year-old Ann Lee showed her schoolwork to her father, he was immediately struck by the excellence of her rendition of a man in the picture. She started to explain the drawing, but before she could finish, her father began hugging her to show his pleasure in her work.

"Dad, don't!" she protested. "I'm trying to tell you something."

Her father then backed off and focused his attention on her words. After listening carefully as she explained what her picture was about, he told his smiling daughter, "You have a lot of good ideas. I like that you shared them with me."

Reflections

Ann's father seemed to realize quickly that, although Ann liked hugs and other physical forms of attention, in this instance she wanted recognition for her ideas. Praising Ann's "good ideas" most likely would have enhanced her self-confidence. Expressing appreciation for sharing the ideas was an encouragement for Ann to share more with him in the future.

Guidelines for Building Self-Esteem

- Be generous in praising your children for their ideas. Also reward them for their creativity and willingness to share their ideas with you.

- Be open to the expressed needs and interests of young children—they may be different than what you first think they are.

The Big Payoff

he parents of Bob and George Walker regularly scolded their six- and nine-year-old boys for not carrying out what was expected of them around the house. Coats were not hung up when the children came in, beds were not made, and their table manners were not up to par. Finally, the Walkers got fed up and decided to institute some new rules. Using an idea they had picked up from a kindergarten teacher, they negotiated a reward and pay-back system to stimulate the kind of behavior they desired. They also hoped the system would reduce the need for reprimands.

They posted a schedule of responsibilities and rewards and offered a nickel for each task accomplished. If the kids were well mannered at dinner, they earned a nickel. Drying the dishes, vacuuming the dining room, and making beds also earned each of them a nickel. All totaled, their responsibilities could earn them each about a dollar a week. On the other hand, if they didn't complete the expected job, they had to pay back a nickel.

The boys leaped at the opportunity to earn some "free" spending money, performing as never before and sometimes even competing to do a task.

Payoff was on Saturday. The Walkers sometimes had to scrape up the required number of nickels, but it was worth it. After getting paid, the boys could immediately go to a store and buy something they "badly needed."

This program dramatically improved the boys' behavior, and it added to family excitement since the boys discussed what they were going to buy. Most important, the number of reprimands decreased significantly.

Reflections

The Walker's used a system of reinforcement to encourage appropriate behavior. While some might wonder whether parents should have to pay their children to behave responsibly, it seemed appropriate here, because of the age and level of maturity of the two boys. Later on, habit and a fuller sense of responsibility would take over, making financial reinforcement unnecessary.

Several points can be made about the incentive system. Because nickels are a form of concrete reinforcement, they were appropriate for the boys' developmental level. Also, the parents were careful to specify clearly what had to be done to earn a nickel. Finally, by permitting the boys to spend their money soon after they earned it, they increased the potency of the reward. After several weeks, however, the parents might have encouraged the boys to save some of the nickels for a more expensive item.

Guidelines for Building Self-Esteem

- Use concrete reinforcements rather than reprimands as incentives to help your young children learn to behave responsibly.
- Since it is difficult for younger children to defer their gratifications, reward desired behavior immediately.

The Cat Came Back

One evening, on his way to a musical program at school, seven-year-old Stephen Johnson announced to his parents that he was going to be one of the five soloists to sing the class song, "The Cat Came Back." What a surprise to his parents!

When it came time for Stephen to take his turn singing a verse, he stepped confidently to the microphone and belted out the first two lines like a pro. Then disaster struck: he couldn't remember the rest of the words. For what seemed like an eternity to his parents, Stephen stared into the audience while the accompanist kept playing "um pa pa, um pa pa." Finally, in a flash of recovery, the cat came back, Stephen remembered his words, and he finished the song with a flourish. The audience immediately gave him a warm and well-deserved round of applause.

When his parents went to meet him after the program, they gave him a big hug and told him what a good job he had done. His father added, "Stephen, I was proud of the way you hung in there and remembered your words."

On the way home, Stephen's mother asked him if he would like to sing a solo again sometime. He said, with genuine interest, "Yeah, I would."

Reflections

It was unfortunate that Stephen's parents didn't know he was going to perform as a soloist. If they had, they could have helped him prepare for his assignment. But, given the situation, the accompanist structured for success by giving Stephen sufficient time to recover and "succeed." And his parents gave him strong positive reinforcement in a situation clouded with some failure. By telling Stephen that they were proud of the way he persevered, they reinforced the quality of fortitude and helped Stephen feel he was capable.

One last point. Children don't always judge failure the same way adults do. Stephen may not have thought that he had done poorly. In fact, he seemed interested in being a soloist again sometime.

Guidelines for Building Self-Esteem

- Recognize that children often have feelings of success even when adults judge that they have failed.
- Find something positive to reinforce when you perceive that your children have not been totally successful at a task.

"You're Right"

Sitting at the snack table eating crackers, eight-year-old Mary Donahue said to her sister Jill, "Crackers and bread are the same." Mary's father quickly interrupted, "No, they're really quite different. Bread has yeast in it that makes it rise but crackers don't, so they stay flat."

Realizing that he may have corrected her too quickly, Mary's father amended his statement by saying, "Sorry, Mary. You're right. They're both made out of flour, and we eat crackers and bread with other foods. In a way, crackers and bread are alike."

111

Reflections

Parents have many occasions to accept or reject their children's ideas or observations. For the sake of their self-esteem, we need to confirm what is correct or right about what our children say and do rather than what is wrong. Talking with his daugher, Mary's father saw an opportunity to be positive and correct his course of communication.

Guidelines for Building Self-Esteem

- Develop a positive rather than a negative frame of mind for responding to what your children say and do. Confirm them as being right whenever you can.
- Ignore errors that are insignificant or can be corrected more effectively at a later time.

"We Sure Do Have Talented Kids in Our Family"

Jon Edberg, an eight-year-old, persistently pounded away on the piano until he was able to hammer out "Silent Night." His mother, wanting to compliment him, yet sensitive to the effect of the compliment on Jon's two less musically talented brothers, said, "Jon, that was terrific. We sure do have talented kids in our family."

Reflections

Jon's mother was rightfully concerned about the effect that complimenting Jon might have on his brothers. She skillfully reinforced Jon for his achievement and reinforced his brothers at the same time. The logic of her statement was that (a) Jon had done a good job and (b) his achievement provided further evidence that the family had talented kids.

Guidelines for Building Self-Esteem

- Compliment your children for their accomplishments. They can't get enough positive strokes.
- Find ways to reinforce directly or indirectly all of your children as you compliment one of them.

"Always So Sloppy"

Ten-year-old Charlie Myers was heartily consuming his spaghetti one evening when noodles started flip-flopping everywhere. Some landed on his shirt, others in his lap. Unable to bear the mess any longer, his mother complained, "Charlie, why are you always so sloppy? Sit up to the table and lean over your plate. Why did you wear that white shirt today anyway? I don't especially enjoy doing five loads of laundry every day."

Charlie made a few hostile adjustments and then continued eating.

Reflections

It is easy to identify with Charlie's mother as she expressed weariness about her workload. But her response to Charlie was inappropriate.

By saying that Charlie was always sloppy, his mother risked turning her complaint into a self-fulfilling prophecy. She also unfairly scolded him for wearing a white shirt. If she knew he was prone to spill, she should have structured the situation for success by having him cover his white shirt with a napkin or towel. Finally, she put an additional burden of guilt on Charlie by complaining about her laundry work.

This combination of rejections could explain Charlie's hostile response. A pattern of parental rejections produces low self-esteem in a child.

Guidelines for Building Self-Esteem

- Do not use all-encompassing words such as "always" or "never" when responding to unacceptable behavior. Deal with each situation specifically. For example, say, "Your hands are not clean. Please wash them" rather than "Why do you *always* have to come to the table with dirty hands?"
- Limit the number of reprimands you offer at any given time.
- Do not discipline by overburdening your children with guilt.

Teens

Not a Carbon Copy

Julie Cohen, a blossoming fourteen-year-old, was enrolled in a private boarding school because she felt she didn't fit in well at the school near her home. Her aunt and uncle, who lived near the private school, wanted to be supportive of Julie during her first week away from her family, so they invited her to stay overnight with them and get reacquainted. They hadn't seen her for two years.

During their visit, her uncle kept noting how much Julie looked and acted like her mother. Julie didn't say much in response, except to point out that her mother's skin was a little lighter than hers. During lunch the next day, however, her uncle continued, "I still can't get over how much you look like your mother. I remember her as a freshman in college—she was only a few years older than you are now. You look just like she did then." Julie flushed a bit and covered her face with her hands as if to say, "I can't take any more of this being compared to my mother."

Reflections

While Julie's uncle may have been understandably surprised to see how much she had grown to look like her mother, mentioning it so many times presented a problem for Julie. Most teenagers are keenly sensitive about their appearance, and they are eager to develop their own identity. Julie didn't feel comfortable being judged to be a carbon copy of her mother. While her uncle thought he was complimenting his niece, he was really denying her individuality and reducing her sense of self-worth.

Guidelines for Building Self-Esteem

- Be aware of the sensitivities and insecurities that teenagers have about their appearance.
- Reinforce teenagers as unique persons by focusing on their individuality rather than by comparing them with other family members. This will help them develop their own identity.

"We Can't Go on Grounding Him Forever"

rank Schrader opened a note from his sixteen-year-old son's English teacher. The note stated that for the fifth day in a row Jim had failed to turn in his homework.

Frank's first impulse was to ground Jim, but then he decided not to take action until he had an opportunity to discuss the problem with his wife, Diane.

In their discussion Diane Schrader came up with the idea that instead of grounding Jim, they might get better results if they involved him in solving his problem. Drawing on a management technique she had used as a schoolteacher, Diane proposed that Jim be required in writing to (1) describe the homework problem from his perspective, including what he thought caused it; (2) describe the problem from his teacher's perspective; and (3) suggest what he thought should be done to solve the problem.

"I like that suggestion," responded her husband. "I guess we can't go on grounding him forever. Let's try it."

Reflections

Involving Jim in solving his problem would be an indirect way of reinforcing him as capable. It would also provide him with the kind of experience that fosters self-discipline and a sense of responsibility for one's behavior.

Guidelines for Building Self-Esteem

- Whenever possible, help adolescents solve their own problems. Doing so will reinforce them as capable of managing their own affairs.
- Praise your teenagers for becoming involved in and solving their own problems.

"Why Has Ted Become So Self-Centered?"

Seventeen-year-old Ted spent so much time at his girlfriend's house that his father thought her family should declare him as an exemption on their income tax form. His mother became so fed up with the situation that on one occasion she said to Ted, "You might as well move in with Jill's family. You're over there most of the time."

In addition to being gone a lot, Ted seemed so self-centered regarding his activities and schedule. He thought that other family members should rearrange their plans so he could use the car; he seemed to have little time for work around the house; he didn't care to join in family activities; and he spent lavishly on his girlfriend's Christmas present but very little on his parent's. On top of everything else, his room was a big mess.

Ted's behavior stimulated his parents to say to themselves, "Why has Ted become so self-centered?"

Reflections

Many of us can readily identify with Ted's parents in this account. It is frustrating to watch our children become so self-centered in

117

adolescence as they move toward independence. We must, however, recognize that their self-focused behavior is normal and even necessary. Being self-focused allows adolescents to turn their attention away from the emotional pain of separating from the family and toward something more pleasurable. The process is similar to reducing physical pain by focusing attention away from it.

Instead of being so critical, it is important for parents to tell their children that they enjoy having them as part of the family and at the same time are pleased to see how much progress they are making toward managing their own affairs. It would also be reasonable for them, without a lot of anger, to negotiate agreements with their teenagers for carrying out their share of the family responsibilities.

Just as in earlier stages of development, parents need to cultivate an attitude of "This, too, shall pass" in relating to the self-focused behavior of adolescents.

Guidelines for Building Self-Esteem

- Avoid being overly critical of teenagers' self-focused behavior as they strive for independence. Rather, reinforce them for the progress they are making toward growing up.
- Let your teenagers know you enjoy being with them and that they will always have a place in your heart when they are away.
- While it is appropriate on occasion to point out a specific self-centered behavior to your teenagers, don't nag at them about it. Nagging will only reinforce their behavior and negate their self-esteem.

"We're Proud of You"

Brad's soccer season had its share of disappointments. As a junior he had won the all-school soccer skills competition and had looked forward to being on the varsity team during his senior year. The coach, however, had other ideas. Brad was relegated to junior varsity for over half of the season and played only sporadically on the varsity during the latter part of the season.

During the last varsity game of the year, Brad's team was behind zero to three with two minutes left. At that point it seemed to many parents that the seniors who had not played much during the year should have been allowed to play the remainder of the game. But the coach did not put them in.

Recognizing that soccer had always been Brad's main sport and that it now had ended on a sour note, his parents stopped on their way home and purchased a box of Brad's favorite candy and a card on which they wrote, "Dear Brad, We admired you for not leading a senior attack on the coach after the game today. We were also upset he did not play the seniors. We have liked your good sportsmanship and leadership throughout the season, both on and off the field. As always, you have made us proud! Love, Mom and Dad."

Reflections

When children are young, they tend to get lots of hugs and kisses as well as attention for their physical and intellectual growth. We mark their increase in height on the wall and post their art work on the refrigerator. When they become teenagers, we tend to reduce these types of reinforcements and fail to replace them with others that are appropriate.

We need to find creative ways to show teenagers they are valued. Writing them a positive message and giving them an unexpected token of appreciation are two good ways to do this.

Guidelines for Building Self-Esteem

- In both good times and bad, reinforce your children as lovable and capable through physical as well as verbal expressions of your thoughts and feelings for them.

Communication Skills for Reinforcing Children as Lovable and Capable

What follows are important skills for reinforcing children as lovable and capable. Examples of what you *might* say in executing each skill are also included.

- **Be specific when you praise your children.** For example:

   Say: You did an excellent job of making your bed. The corners are tucked in neatly and there are no wrinkles.
   Say: I like the way you said "please" and "thank you" at Aunt Nancy's last night.

- **Be specific when you reprimand your children.** For example:

Say: You slammed the door. Next time close it gently.

Say: You played out on the street. I want you to stay on this side of the sidewalk.

- **Generalize about the positive traits or abilities your children exhibit repeatedly.** For example:

Say: I love to hear you play the clarinet so well. I think you have great musical talent.

Say: You sewed the hem on the skirt very evenly. I think you're good with your hands.

- **Avoid generalizing about what children do that is incorrect or inappropriate.** For example:

Don't say: You're *always* so sloppy.

Don't say: I wish you could *just once* hang up your clothes.

- **Reinforce your children for who they are as well as what they can do.** For example:

Say: I really enjoy being with you.

Say: I'm glad you're my daughter.

Say: Our family wouldn't be complete without you.

- **Convey to your children that you love them even though you don't like what they have done.** For example:

Say: I love you, and for that reason I can't let you stay out as late as you did last night.

Say: (As you gently put your hand on your child's shoulder) Let's think of a better way to express your feelings than kicking your bicycle.

- **Focus on their behavior rather than the children themselves when reprimanding them.** For example:

  Don't say: I've had it with you dragging mud into the house.
  Say: Walking into the kitchen with muddy shoes tracks dirt in. Please take off your shoes before coming in.

  Don't say: You little sneak. You lied to me about turning in your homework.
  Say: You told me that your homework was done, but your teacher called and said you didn't turn it in yesterday.

  Don't say: Mr. Irresponsible! You always leave your bike in the driveway when I want to park the car in the garage.
  Say: You left your bike in the driveway, and I had to get out of the car and put it away before I could park in the garage. Please put your bike away next time.

- **Use feeling statements to reinforce positive traits or behaviors of your children.** For example:

  Say: I really feel happy when you share your toys.
  Say: I feel proud that you earned the achievement award in your music class.

- **Reinforce some aspect of your children's performance in situations of apparent failure.** For example:

  Say: (In response to a child's incorrect answer) Nice try!
  Say: (In response to a hastily drawn painting) I like the bright colors you have used.

Developmental Needs of Children That Should Be Considered in Applying the Reinforcement Skills

How you reinforce younger, less mature children as capable and lovable will differ from how you reinforce older, more mature children.

Younger, less mature children need:

- concrete, physical tokens of your love for them and approval of their efforts (such as cookies, stickers, and trips to baseball games).
- rewards that are regular and immediate.
- reinforcement for even the slightest bit of appropriate behavior.
- reinforcement that they are lovable by showing them that they are capable.

Older, more mature children need:

- more abstract and verbal reinforcement, such as expressions of appreciation, approval, and love.
- deferred rewards, such as a trip later on or a party in the future.
- reinforcement for their social, emotional, and intellectual development.
- expressions of love apart from your judgements about what they can or cannot do.

Summary

We've stressed in this chapter the importance of displaying a positive attitude toward our children. We need to reinforce what we find right rather than what we find wrong about their behavior. We also need to be generous with praise, rewards, and encouragement.

Putting this principle into practice does not mean that we never correct our children's behavior. Their growth depends on sound teaching as well as on praise and encouragement. We need to correct our children at times to help them grow and develop, but we should generally take a positive approach and offer lots of positive reinforcement for appropriate behavior. By reinforcing our children as lovable and capable, we strengthen their self-esteem.

*In building self-esteem,
it is more effective to
reinforce what we find right
about our children's behavior
than to nag about
what we find wrong.*

Model a Positive View of Yourself to Your Children

Children of all ages learn by observing others and then trying to imitate them. Research shows that children who view aggressive behavior tend to become aggressive themselves. Children who are abused by their parents tend to become child abusers.

But children not only imitate what others do and how they do it, they also imitate the personal traits of the people they observe, including their level of self-esteem. Whether we intend it or not, the degree to which we like ourselves influences the degree to which our children like themselves.

Since self-esteem can, to a degree, be "caught" from parents, we need actively and intentionally to display (or "model") to our children positive attitudes about ourselves. This includes being willing to talk about our strengths (as well as areas where we need improvement) and to take care not to continually run ourselves down.

The vignettes that follow highlight what you should and should not do to model self-esteem to your children.

Early Childhood

Let It All Hang Out

O ne thing could be said with confidence about thirteen-month-old Beth: she was not depressed. Her bright eyes and broad smile radiated the sunshine of life to all who had the opportunity to behold her.

Her mother, Jean, also possessing a sparkling countenance, loved to play freely with Beth. They laughed heartily together when Jean would let Beth push her over on the floor and sit on her, or when Jean would impulsively knock over a stack of blocks that they had just built up. Jean "let it all hang out" with Beth and Beth loved it.

Reflections

Jean's play with Beth not only reinforced Beth's natural playfulness as OK, but it also provided a model of a care-giver who was personally secure enough to step out of her adult role and be spontaneous and impulsive. It also demonstrated to Beth that her mother was capable of meeting her needs for amusement. While Beth at her age could not understand all this, she undoubtedly benefited from her mother's indirect way of modeling self-esteem.

Guidelines for Building Self-Esteem

- Model self-esteem to small children by freely and confidently entering their world of play.

The Scary Room

Carlos, an otherwise emotionally healthy three-year-old, seemed to have only one ongoing source of anxiety in his life: for some reason, he had developed a fear of going into the laundry room in the basement.

One day, a toy car that he had been playing with rolled into the scary room. "Mom," he cried, "My car rolled into the laundry room, and I'm scared to go in there."

Carlos's mother responded, "That room is a bit scary for you, isn't it. Let me get you car for you."

Reflections

Carlos's mother was wise in empathizing with her son's fear. To have called his reaction "silly" or to have forced him to enter the room would have belittled his feelings and reduced his sense of self-worth. That she freely volunteered to enter the room modeled a sense of personal security to him. Demonstrating personal security is a way of modeling self-esteem.

Guidelines for Building Self-Esteem

- Without putting your children down for their fears, model that you are not afraid to face the challenges that life presents.

"Man, Are You Handsome!"

While shaving one morning, Tom Willis noticed a small head appear in the lower corner of the mirror. His five-year-old daughter, Wendy, had come in to keep him company.

Pretending not to notice her, Tom said to himself as he looked in the mirror, "How'd you get to be so good looking? Man, are you handsome!" Wendy laughed and pleaded in a "don't-kid-me" tone, "Dad . . . !"

Appearing startled, her father responded, "Well, aren't I? And you should be glad. That's how you got to be so pretty—from your good-looking mom and dad." Wendy smiled contentedly.

Reflections

Tom wanted to convey to Wendy his sense of self-confidence and self-worth, and he did it in a lighthearted way. His comments modeled a positive attitude toward himself, as well as toward others in the family. Because Wendy was at a relatively dependent stage of childhood, it was especially important that her father provide a confident and positive picture of himself.

Guidelines for Building Self-Esteem

- Give your children an opportunity to see that you genuinely seem happy with yourself and are not afraid to occasionally recognize, in a fun rather than conceited way, some of your own virtues.

Middle Childhood

"Nobody's Perfect"

Annie Blake was as likely as any seven-year-old to conclude that when she failed at a specific task, she was a failure in general. One evening when her mother, Colleen, was at her desk in the den, Annie appeared at her side and asked her what she was doing.

Colleen answered, "Writing some things for work, honey."

Annie looked at the page she was working on. "What are these?" she asked.

Her mother replied, "Those are mistakes. I wrote the wrong words, so I had to cross them out and change them."

Surprised, Annie pressed on, "But you have five of them on this page. That's a lot."

In a casual tone, her mother said, "Oh, I don't know. I'd say most people would make that many. Everyone makes mistakes—nobody's perfect. What's important is that you're not afraid to see and to correct them. Even you super-kids make mistakes, don't you?"

Annie agreed, "Yeah—I make mistakes at school."

Giving her a big hug, Colleen said, "Well, you do a great job at school. A mistake now and then is OK, right? What's more, I love you whether you make mistakes or not."

Reflections

Seeing that Annie was suprised that she made mistakes, her mother capitalized on the opportunity to neutralize the message that you have to be perfect in order to feel good about yourself. She attempted to model realistic expectations that would help Annie's self-esteem in the future. She also focused positively on recognizing and correcting errors, rather than on the errors themselves.

Guidelines for Building Self-Esteem

- Show your children that "to err is human" and that they should feel good about themselves in spite of the mistakes they make.
- Focus positively on correcting mistakes and solving problems rather than on the mistakes and problems themselves.

"I Can Be Helpful"

One Saturday morning, Helen Reese announced to her children that she was going next door to help a neighbor do some redecorating. Seven-year-old Willy asked, "Why are you doing that?"

Helen paused. "Well, I'm good at wallpapering so I know I can be helpful. And I want to help."

Reflections

Helen Reese showed her children that it is OK to talk positively about your abilities. She also demonstrated that she was secure enough about herself to reach out freely to help a neighbor. In addition, when she came back from doing the job, she could show her children the satisfaction gained from doing something for someone else, which would only heighten the sense of self-esteem she reflected to her children.

Guidelines for Building Self-Esteem

- Talk positively about the talents you possess.
- Show your children that you are concerned about helping others. Doing so is an indirect means of modeling self-esteem.

"Oh, My Aching Back"

As usual, the dinner conversation at the Nelsons' was dominated by Chuck Nelson's complaints to his wife and children about his health. His hay fever was worse than ever, and his low back pain had returned. As he left the table for a rest on the couch, he fretted, "I hope the onions don't give me indigestion."

Reflections

Chuck's overemphasis on his physical ailments probably taught his children to focus on their own ailments and helped make them feel insecure. By constantly harping on his condition, he unintentionally modeled poor self-esteem.

Guidelines for Building Self-Esteem

- Be careful about how often you highlight your aches and pains, or your worries, within your family.
- If you do talk about your physical, mental, or emotional problems, focus on gains made or improvements anticipated.

133

"Let's Give Mom a Hug"

I t was 6:25 P.M. and Cindy Jensen was due home from work. Her husband, Dan, was home working at his desk, and their children, Patti and Todd, ages six and eight, were watching TV.

When their father recognized the familiar sound of Cindy's car entering the driveway, he called out to the children, "I'll bet your mother would like a 'welcome home' kiss. How about it if we all run and greet her at the door?" Todd and Patti chimed in, "OK!"

Dan was right: Cindy was pleasantly surprised, and she rewarded them all with hugs and words of praise for the "welcome home."

During the next two days, the family welcomed her home the same way; then the ritual began to taper off. But Dan was able to revive it quite easily by modeling and reminding the kids that their mom loved such displays of affection.

Reflections

Patti and Todd were both at an age where they thought about themselves more than they thought about others and what their needs might be. Dan not only encouraged his children to display affection toward their mother, he also modeled it himself. He sensed that such attention would contribute to his wife's self-esteem and to positive relationships among other family members.

Guidelines for Building Self-Esteem

- Encourage your children to follow your example of showing love and concern for other family members. Doing so will give them a sense of satisfaction and accomplishment, and it will boost their own self-esteem in the long run.
- Parents should devise ways to maintain and enhance each other's self-esteem.

Fire Fright

Brian and Susan Martin had decided to establish fire-escape procedures for their family. One evening at dinner, Brian announced his intentions to his sons, ages nine and eleven. The older boy responded enthusiastically, "Dad, let me help! We studied this in school. A fireman came to our class and—"

His father interrupted, "No, I'll handle this. This is not kid's stuff. Have you ever seen a charred body taken out of a burning building? It's not a pretty sight. It's possible that we could have a fire, so listen carefully."

By now both boys were fearful and quiet.

Reflections

Brian did not need to frighten his children in order to impress upon them the dangers of fire. Alarming them, as he did, most likely made them feel less secure and less confident. He could have calmly described what happens when a fire breaks out and then explained how to escape from a burning house. He could also have eased the threat of a fire by allowing the children to contribute ideas about what to do and then having them thoroughly practice the procedures.

Guidelines for Building Self-Esteem

- Do not transmit personal fears to children when you're issuing warnings or planning for their safety. Teach, don't terrorize.
- Involve your children in planning family activities, whenever possible. Doing so will not only give them a greater stake in the plans but will also demonstrate that you feel secure enough about yourself to be open to their ideas.

"I Know I Can Do It"

The Goldberg family (including Ari, twelve, and Becky, ten) was going to sing in a musical program at their synagogue. Ari and Becky's father, Sol, had been asked to be a soloist.

Every chance he had, he practiced his song. As he practiced, he would point out to his children that in order to do a good job, one has to be well prepared. To bolster his own self-confidence and model a positive attitude, he told them, as Louis Pasteur had said in a book they had recently read, "I can do it. I know I can do it."

During the program Sol showed that, in fact, he could do it. The program was a big success, and he sang like a pro.

Reflections

The Goldbergs had an excellent opportunity to model self-esteem as they participated in the musical program with their children. Sol Goldberg's self-confidence demonstrated the importance of thinking and speaking positively. By relating his "I-can-do-it" attitude to one of the children's stories, he reinforced the point even more strongly. From his example, his children could also learn that being thoroughly prepared can lead to success, which could only increase their self-confidence.

Sol's success in the program illustrated the benefits of having self-esteem. Had he made some goofs, however, he would still have had an opportunity to model positive self-regard to his children by indicating that it's OK to make some mistakes.

Guidelines for Building Self-Esteem

- Model a positive attitude to your children by making positive statements about your capabilities.
- Show how thorough preparation can lead to success.
- Let your children know that you feel OK about yourself even when you've made a mistake.

Teens

"We Were Good Kids"

One evening Kate Redfern was showing her children some pictures of her in junior high. When Kevin, her fifteen-year-old, saw what his mother was wearing, he said, "Look how puffy your skirt is. Were you that fat?"

"No," explained Kate. "All the girls in my group wore what we called can-can slips. They made our skirts puff out."

Thirteen-year-old Dawn then noted how all of her mother's friends looked alike. They all had pony tails, bobby socks, and black-and-white saddle shoes. Her mother smiled and said, "It was fun being part of a group. We were good kids."

Reflections

Because we don't want our children to be negatively influenced by peer-group pressure, we often encourage them to think and act for themselves. This is a good goal to shoot for, but it may not be reasonable for adolescents in all situations. Developing youngsters have a strong need to belong; satisfying that need can help them move toward independent thought and action. Kate Redfern's pictures helped her show her children that it is all right and even fun to belong to a peer group.

Guidelines for Building Self-Esteem

- Show your children that it's normal and enjoyable to be part of a peer group.
- Rather than constantly rejecting children for wanting to be like their peers, reinforce their interests in doing so. (This assumes, of course, that the peer-group behavior does not violate any of your basic values.)

Mr. Positive

Sam Rinaldi, father of fourteen-year-old Tony and sixteen-year-old Angie, was known to his family and friends as "Mr. Positive." When frustration, failure, or disaster came his way, he expressed his negative feelings freely and then quickly bounced back with an optimistic response. Several examples come to mind.

One day when Sam realized that he would have to return home from work because Tony's baseball uniform was left in the car, he said, "Rats!" But then he thought to himself, "This is an opportunity to show Tony I love him." He told him so as he handed the uniform to him. When Angie broke up with her boyfriend, he told her how sorry he felt and then helped her see there would be plenty of good times ahead. When the spring on the garage door broke and the door came crashing down on top of the car, he said to his family, "This is terrible, but it's a good thing it didn't happen when one of us was under it."

In every way, Sam was a picture of brightness and hope to his family.

Reflections

By modeling a positive disposition to his children, Sam indirectly modeled self-esteem. This is so because he could not have been genuinely positive unless he felt secure enough about himself to believe that he counted and that life had something good in store for him.

Sam also gave his children a sense of hope by exhibiting a positive attitude. Our children so desperately need hope as they live in a world they often see as threatening and bewildering. In fact, without hope our children cannot feel very good about themselves.

Guidelines for Building Self-Esteem

- While it is appropriate to express negative feelings in a responsible way, look for ways to model a positive perspective to your children. Doing so will help build self-esteem.

"I Share Your Concern"

Teens Jill and Tom Ross were in the family room with their father when their mother came home from work. Their mom had had one of those "bad days" we all have occasionally. Tired and irritable, she remarked to her husband, "I thought you were going to mow the lawn. It looks terrible, and we're having company tomorrow!"

Giving her a little hug, her husband responded empathetically, "I share your concern. How would you feel if I mowed the lawn right after supper?"

"I suppose that's OK," replied his wife. "But I feel strongly that it needs to be done before tomorrow."

After their parents had gone to the kitchen, Jill turned to Tom and said, "It's kinda neat how mom and dad support each other. Last week when dad was grouchy, mom didn't take it personally or let it get her down. She just listened to him and offered encouragement.

Reflections

Their father's response to his wife's criticism showed Jill and Tom that he was able to handle the conflict without experiencing self-doubt or becoming defensive. It also showed that he was sensitive to her feelings.

Guidelines for Building Self-Esteem

- Model self-esteem to your children by reacting securely and nondefensively to criticism.

"Can't You See His Face?"

Megan and Dan Ellis went with their parents to the annual junior high school carnival. A drawing was held and their father won the door prize, a deluxe fishing rod.

"You sure can have fun with this, Dad," said Megan.

"Yeah," replied her father, "but I think I'll give it to Uncle Mark. He's much more of a fisherman than I am, and he's got an old, beat-up rod. Can't you just see his face when I give it to him?"

Reflections

What Megan and Dan's father did will have more effect on helping his children be generous than a hundred admonitions to "share your things," "be generous," and "think of others." Constantly urging children to think of others and then rejecting them when they don't can only damage their self-esteem. Modeling concern for others and praising children for the least amount of it they exhibit helps them learn to be considerate of others and indirectly enhances their self-esteem.

Guidelines for Building Self-Esteem

- Show your children that there is joy and pleasure in thinking of others. Doing so will stimulate them to be generous, too.
- Avoid chipping away at children for their selfishness. Instead, praise them for the least bit of generosity they show.

Developmental Needs of Children That Should Be Considered in Applying the Modeling Principle

Younger, less mature children need:

- parents who model that they are capable as well as lovable. (Young children need this because at their level of development they assign great worth to being capable.)
- concrete demonstrations from parents that they possess self-confidence and self-respect.

Older, more mature children need:

- parents who view themselves as lovable, even though they show that they are not capable in some areas of their lives.
- verbal expressions from parents that they like themselves.

Summary

The principle of "modeling" self-esteem is perhaps the most critical of all the principles we've discussed, since, to a degree, children "catch" their sense of self-esteem from their parents.

While you cannot completely control how you feel about yourself, you can attempt to control your behavior. You can talk positively about yourself, act in self-confident ways, and reinforce others for doing the same.

All of us, to some degree, feel less than satisfied with who we are and what we can do. But for the sake of our own self-esteem and that of our children, we should try to break the habit of constantly talking negatively about ourselves. One avenue to self-improvement is to begin to think and talk positively about ourselves.

As we carry out this principle, we need to display a positive (but not conceited) attitude. While we may occasionally admit that we need to improve in one area or another, we must focus on what is good about ourselves and express that good to our children. We must also point out the good in others and express the hope that the shortcomings we reveal to our children or observe in others can be corrected. Showing that we feel good about ourselves will help our children feel good about themselves.

Since self-esteem can, to a degree, be caught from adults, we need to talk and act in ways that show our children we feel lovable and capable.

PART II

Putting the Principles of Self-Esteem into Action

We have emphasized in Part I five principles for helping children grow up with high self-esteem. In this final section we'll present some ways to put these principles into operation. First, we'll discuss some attitudes that might be inhibiting you from concentrating on the self-esteem of your children; then we'll outline a systematic plan to help you improve your efforts at building their self-esteem.

Attitudes to Overcome

If you're like most of us, habit impedes your efforts to change the way you think and behave. So if you want to do more to help your children, you'll have to identify the attitudes that habitually get in the way; then develop a plan to change them. Here are some of the most common inhibiting attitudes and suggestions for altering them.

I have to spend so much time teaching my children to behave properly that I don't have time to work on their self-esteem. Anyway, self-esteem will follow if my children are taught to behave.

For some parents, "teaching" quite often means chipping away at their children's flaws. These parents are on their children's backs from morning until night, believing that by shaping the "perfect child," they'll raise children who will feel good about themselves. For these parents, self-esteem is a by-product of teaching good behavior and dependent on being perfect.

We believe, however, that parents can teach their children good behavior and build their self-esteem at the same time and that children do not need to be perfect in order to feel good about themselves. The kind of teaching we're talking about considers the needs, interest, and abilities of children; encourages, supports, and reinforces them as they go about learning; and carries with it a respect for the dignity and worth of each child. Self-esteem should not simply be a by-product of teaching; it should be one of its major products.

As we teach our children, we must avoid being unnecessarily judgmental, overly critical, and impatient. Statements such as "You're doing it wrong again" or "Can't you do anything right?" or "How many times do I have to tell you?" have devastating effects on children's self-esteem. Instead, we ought to teach our children by modeling the correct behavior, reinforcing the positive aspects of what they're doing, describing specifically what they have done wrong and what they should be doing, and clearly establishing the consequences of performing correctly or incorrectly. We also need to help them believe that they are capable of learning. This kind of teaching will increase their self-esteem immeasurably.

In short, we believe that it's possible to help our children develop positive self-concepts because it's possible to teach them good behavior and enhance their self-esteem at the same time.

I hesitate doing too much to promote self-esteem in my children because I fear they'll become too self-centered as adults.

Many of us have learned this attitude from our own parents. They may have bragged about us to other parents, but they hardly ever complimented us directly because they didn't want us to get "big heads." At the heart of this attitude is the belief that children will not develop a genuine concern for others if they think too highly of themselves. We all know adults who can focus only on their own needs. To make sure our children don't turn out this way, we tend to overcompensate by trying to make them "socially acceptable" before they're ready. We force our children to be self-less, which leaves them feeling confused, guilty, and inadequate.

To avoid this, should we let children be self-centered? No and yes. While we need not accept behaviors that have negative consequences for others, we should accept their self-focused thinking as natural for them at their stage of development. Seeing our children as innately self-focused will help reduce the amount of anger that we express to them, which in turn will allow us to help them learn to love others as well as themselves. Less anger will also help our children feel more lovable and capable.

We would like to propose three positive approaches to helping children consider others and still feel good about themselves.

1. Provide opportunities for your children to see other, more mature individuals function in a socially acceptable manner. They need to see you display your concern for others. Doing so will cause them to reconsider their own way of thinking and behaving and possibly stimulate them to adopt a more mature approach to life.

   One parent we know recalls that when she asked her young son to run an occasional errand in the house, he would either refuse or say, "Will you play a game of cribbage with me if I do?" She would accept his reaction as typical for his stage of development and perhaps play a game in exchange for the errand. Later, she would occasionally offer to do him a favor, making it clear that she enjoyed doing something for someone she cared for. It was a memorable day when, having requested that he carry some clean clothes from the laundry to his bedroom, he replied, "Sure, Mom, I'd be glad to." When we model concern for others, we stimulate our children to focus on others and indirectly promote their self-esteem.

2. Provide opportunities for your children to realize the pleasure of doing things for others. Participate together in activities that benefit another family member. For instance, when you and one of your children bake a birthday cake for another family member, the child gets to experience the family member's pleasure in the cake, your pleasure in doing something to make that person happy, and the pleasure of sharing the activity with you. You are the crucial element in this experience. The experience won't have the same value if you say, "It's your sister's birthday. Why don't you do something nice and go bake her a cake."

Another way to help our children experience the pleasure of doing something for others is to give them a small amount of money and then help them spend it on other family members. If they are allowed to be "generous' without having it cost them too much, they'll begin to feel the pleasure that generosity brings. As they develop, they will one day say to their parents, "We'll buy Christmas presents with our own money this year. If you give us the money, the gifts really won't be from us."

Lastly, children can realize the pleasure of helping those outside the family through participation in community service activities. Schools, churches, synagogues, and other organizations can help you arrange such experiences.

3. Reinforce any hints of considerate behavior your children display. For example, when your child is willing to trade a toy with another child, reinforce his behavior as "generous." And when your child writes a thank-you note to his grandparents after strong encouragement from you, reinforce his action as "thoughtful." Consideration for the welfare of others can be gradually shaped by a series of positive reinforcements.

While it is appropriate to help children move beyond their self-centeredness by encouraging them to be considerate of others, parents shouldn't expect their children to pour themselves wholeheartedly into it. Accepting our children as OK, even though they're self-focused, is fundamental to helping them mature and feel good about themselves at the same time.

I'm unable to focus on the self-esteem of my children because I feel so overwhelmed myself.

Parents who feel overwhelmed are inhibited from doing as much as they should to enhance the self-esteem of their children. Given all that is expected of them, they often feel so spent and so inadequate that they cannot even carry on a decent conversation with adults. It's difficult for them, they say, to get their brains into gear for anything but mundane, everyday tasks.

There's no single way to attend to our own self-esteem, but we can recommend that you apply the five self-esteem principles to yourself as well as to your children.

- Accept your thoughts and feelings—be aware of them and express them to others.
- Structure your life to maximize chances for success. Don't get involved in too many demanding activities; be clear about your goals; identify sources of help; avoid obstacles; and set reasonable standards for assessing your accomplishments.
- Establish enough control over your life so that you live it more fully. This may require you to plan and organize your daily activities more thoroughly, acquire some new knowledge or skill, deal with a thought or emotion that has you bound, or learn to be more assertive.
- Reinforce yourself as lovable and capable. Talk positively about who you are and what you can do and reward yourself for successful efforts. Resolve not to punish yourself for making unavoidable errors in raising your children. You are only human, and humans make mistakes.

- Surround yourself with friends who can model a positive sense of self-esteem to you. You will gain more strength from those who feel good about themselves than you will from those who drag you down by their low self-esteem.

Putting the Principles of Self-Esteem into Operation

By confronting those attitudes that prevent us from helping our children develop a sense of self-worth, we are taking the first step toward putting the five principles of self-esteem into operation. What follows are suggestions that can help you start applying the self-esteem principles in a systematic way. Try those that feel right for you and that you believe will help you.

- Write the following five statements on cards and read them aloud daily for a month, or even longer:

    1. I listen to and acknowledge the thoughts and feelings of my children.

    2. I structure the environment of my children so they will experience feelings of success, not failure.

    3. I give my children a feeling of reasonable control over their lives.

    4. I reinforce my children as lovable and capable.

    5. I model a positive view of myself to my children.

This may seem simple-minded, but it isn't. Don't underestimate the power of habit. Repeating these principles for a period of time will help you remember and follow them. After a while, you will be more sensitive to occasions when you have and have not applied the principles. Try it and test the results.

- Keep in mind the following key words. They stand for the five self-esteem principles, and they can serve as cues to the way you interact with your children.

Listen and acknowledge

Structure for success

Reasonable control

Reinforce

Model

- To help reinforce constructive behavior, have your spouse or a close friend point out occasions when you've applied one of the self-esteem principles. Later, to increase the number of options you have available to help your children, the two of you might want to talk about alternative ways of carrying out each principle. After that, you can identify a problem you've had in applying one of the principles and then develop a strategy together for solving it. Finally, talking with your spouse or friend about a goal related to one of the five principles will help you clarify the goal and strengthen your commitment to achieve it. Throughout your discussions, you'll make your time together both enlightening and therapeutic if you share your feelings freely.

- Praise your spouse or friends when you see them carrying out any of the five self-esteem principles in an appropriate way. The reinforcement will be good for them and will help you become more aware of applying the principles yourself.
- Talk positively about your capacity to help your children. Speak positively about your potential and your accomplishments. At the least hint of improvement in your performance, say that you are doing better. Before you know it, you will be. You might also want to jot down your significant accomplishments; reading a list of positive efforts can be very encouraging.
- Find at least two other persons interested in this subject and share with them family events that have had positive or negative effects on self-esteem. If you feel so inclined, write up some family situations and interactions as vignettes similar to those in this book and discuss them with your group. Point out what you have learned from these experiences.
- Apply the five self-esteem principles in dealing with your spouse and friends. The more you do, the more you'll be aware of applying them in dealing with your children.
- Take time to relax. Audio tapes are available that talk you through the process of relaxing your body. Engage in activities you enjoy, whether it be reading, fishing, or walking. And keep yourself physically fit. Try an exercise program that helps you stretch tight muscles. These exercises will help you at the end of a trying day. Relaxing and exercising will tune you up to apply the self-esteem principles effectively.
- Read other books and articles on self-esteem. You will find the ideas they offer complement the principles that we have recommended. (See the Suggested Readings at the end of this book.)

Some of these activities will fit you and your schedule better than others. We offer them as suggestions worth trying. Many adults have found them to be helpful.

Self-Esteem and Values

In *Self-Esteem for Tots to Teens* we have emphasized that as parents we can play a significant part in shaping the self-esteem of our children. We also wish to acknowledge that as our children mature into adolescence and beyond, their values play an increasingly important part in shaping how they feel about themselves. Children at these more advanced stages of development will feel good about themselves when they choose to live in accordance with their values, when their values are consistent with each other, and when they hold healthy values that have stood the test of time across many cultures and religions such as honesty, justice, mercy and respect for human dignity. These enduring values will sustain our children both because they are honorable in themselves and because society will reinforce our children when they live in accordance with them. Thus, in addition to following our five principles for building self-esteem in your children, we strongly recommend that you lay the groundwork for helping your children develop a sound set of values.

Conclusion

We began this book with three objectives in mind. We wanted you to

1. understand and accept how children look at the world.

2. know five principles for building self-esteem.

3. know how to apply the principles of self-esteem appropriately as you interact with your children at various stages of their development.

We trust that our book has helped you feel more confident about your ability to build self-esteem in your children. With self-esteem as an energizer, our children will be empowered to lead responsible and fulfilled lives. Self-esteem is one of the greatest gifts you can give your children, a gift they will cherish for a lifetime.

Suggested Readings

On Self-Esteem

Briggs, Dorothy C. *Your Child's Self-Esteem: The Key to Life.* New York: Doubleday, 1970.

Dobson, James. *Hide or Seek.* Old Tappan, N.J.: Revell, 1974.

Clarke, Jean I. *Self-Esteem: A Family Affair.* Minneapolis: Winston, 1978.

On Communicating with Children

Faber, Adele, and Elaine Mazlish. *How to Talk So Kids Will Listen and Listen So Kids Will Talk.* New York: Rawson, Wade, 1980.

Ginott, Haim. *Between Parent and Child.* New York: Macmillan, 1965.

Gordon, Thomas. *Parent Effectiveness Training: The Tested Way to Raise Responsible Children.* New York: McKay, 1970.

On Developmental Psychology

Likona, Thomas. *Raising Good Children.* New York: Bantam, 1983.

Loevinger, Jane, and Ruth Wessler. *Measuring Ego Development.* San Francisco: Jossey-Bass, 1970.

Pearce, Joseph C. *Magical Child.* New York: Dutton, 1977.

Rogers, Carl. *Client-Centered Therapy*. Boston: Houghton Mifflin, 1951.

On Relating Self-Esteem to Education

Beane, James and Lipka, Richard. *Self-Concept, Self-Esteem, and the Curriculum*. Newton, MA: Allyn and Bacon, Inc., 1984.

Glasser, William. *Schools Without Failure*. New York: Harper & Row, 1969.

Purkey, William. *Inviting School Success*. Belmont, Calif.: Wadsworth, 1984.

_____ . *Self-Concept and School Achievement*. Englewood Cliffs, N.J.: Prentice-Hall, 1970.

Rich, Dorothy. *MegaSkills: How Families Can Help Children Succeed in School and Beyond*. Boston: Houghton Mifflin, 1988.

Index

Other Materials Available from Parenting and Teaching Publications

Redman, George L., *Building Self-Esteem in Students: A Skill and Strategy Workbook for Teachers*. Wayzata: Parenting and Teaching Publications, revised edition, 1992.

Based on the five principles for building self-esteem described in *Self-Esteem for Tots to Teens,* this workbook helps teachers to more fully understand and apply skills and strategies for building self-esteem in students. The workbook will help you to

- learn the critical elements of each skill
- recognize an example of the skill
- practice, in writing, how to perform the skill
- work effectively with colleagues in learning and using the skills

As a complement to *Self-Esteem for Tots to Teens*, this "learn-by-doing" workbook has proven useful to individual teachers as well as groups of teachers in staff development workshops and continuing education classes. Guidelines are provided for learning and practicing the skills in small cooperative groups.

Comments about the Workbook:

"I found the workbook to be very clear. I could, at my own pace, complete each exercise and internalize the skill described."

"Several of us discussed the exercises outside of our continuing education class. It was fun and gave me a broader perspective on how and when to use the skills."

"I like the workbook. It made me think about how I was using the skills and how I will use them in the future."

Redman, George L., *Building Self-Esteem in Children: A Skill and Strategy Workbook for Parents.* **Wayzata: Parenting and Teaching Publications, revised edition, 1992.**

Paralleling *Building Self-Esteem in Students,* this version of the workbook has been enthusiastically received by parents, parent educators, and others who care for children.

"I was impressed with the material contained within this workbook. Our staff will find it a useful tool as they work with families."

Dr. Barry Garfinkel, M.D., F.R.C.P. (C)
Director, Child and Adolescent Psychiatry
University of Minnesota

Order Form

Qty.	Title	Order No.	Unit Cost	Total
	Self-Esteem for Tots to Teens By E. Anderson, G. Redman, and C. Rogers	100	8.95	
	Building Self-Esteem in Children: A Skill and Strategy Workbook for Parents. By G. Redman	110	19.95	
	Building Self-Esteem in Students: A Skill and Strategy Workbook for Teachers. By G. Redman	120	19.95	
	Subtotal			
	MN residents add **6.5%** sales tax			
	Shipping and Handling (see below)			
	Total			

Shipping and Handling

Book: Add $1.25 for postage and handling for first book and $.50 for each additional book.

Workbook: Add $2.00 for postage and handling for first workbook and $.75 for each additional workbook.

Canada and Overseas: Add $2.00 to the above shipping and handling charges for books shipped to Canada. Overseas postage will be billed.

Quantity discounts: For orders including six or more items, a 10% discount is available.

Send book(s) to:

Name _____ .

Address _____

City _____ State _____ ZIP _____

Make check or money order payable to:
Parenting and Teaching Publications, 16686 Meadowbrook Lane, Wayzata, MN 55391.
Phone orders: (612) 473-1793